Intuitive Entrepreneurship

Babak Soltanian

Copyright © 2017 by Babak Soltanian

This publication is sold with the understanding that the author is not engaged in rendering legal, accounting or other professional services. If legal advice or other expert assistance is required, the services of a professional person should be sought.

All rights reserved. No part of this publication may be reproduced, distributed, or transmitted in any form or by any means, including photocopying, recording, or other electronic or mechanical methods, without the prior written permission of the author, except in the case of brief quotations embodied in critical reviews and certain other noncommercial uses permitted by copyright law.

ISBN: 9781976737831

First Edition

For Mom and Dad

Table of Contents

Preface **1**

Introduction **5**

Chapter On: What You Are Getting Into **13**
   Having a Realistic Vision 13
   The Mental Game 15
   Having Sufficient Bandwidth 16
   Having Conviction 19
   Staying Authentic and Genuine 21
   Ethics and Principles 22
   Managing Oneself 24
   Networking 26
   Outcomes 28

Chapter Two: Business Plan **31**
   Fundamentals 32
      Product & Technology 32
      Customer Base 34
      Customer Acquisition 37
      Market Size 40
      Scalability 43
      Sales Channels 45
      Competition 48
      Team 53
      Unfair Advantage 56
      Revenue Model & Margins 58
   Prototype & Feasibility 60
   Budget Estimate 61
   Corporate Social Responsibility 64
   Pulling the Trigger 65

Chapter Three: Structure **69**
   Legal Considerations 69
   Legal Entities 73
      C Corporation 75

- S Corporation 76
- Limited Liability Company 78
- Partnership 80
- Sole Proprietorship 80
- Cooperative 81
- Incorporation Flow Chart 82
- Board of Directors 83
- Patents & Intellectual Property 85
- Organization Chart 92

Chapter Four: Equity Dilemmas 93
- Co-founders and Employees 97
- Advisors 99
- Board Members 100
- Investors 100
  - Convertible Notes 102
  - Venture Round 104

Chapter Five: Fundraising 111
- Before Approaching Investors 112
  - What investors look for 112
  - Non-Disclosure Agreement 113
  - Do Your Homework 115
  - Exit Strategy 115
  - Know Your Investor 116
- Pitch Material 119
  - Elevator Pitch 119
  - One-Page Executive Summary 121
  - Summary Slide Deck 125
  - Main Slide Deck 128
- Sources of Capital 129
  - Bootstrapping 130
  - Friends & Family 132
  - Crowdfunding 134
  - Incubators 136
  - Angel Investors 138
  - Venture Capital 139
  - Corporate Ventures 146
  - Government Grants 148

    Small Business Administration Loans 153
Chapter Six: Operations **155**
    Initial Expenses 155
    Registrations & Licenses 156
    Tracking progress 157
    Record Keeping 158
    Finance & Accounting 160
        Taxes 161
        Bank Accounts & Credit Cards 162
    Online Presence 163
        Website 163
        Email 165
        Social Media 165
    Human Resources 166
        Hiring 166
        Firing Employees 168
        Motivating Your Team 170
    Office Space 171
    Business Cards 173

Chapter Seven: Next Steps **175**
    Pivot 175
    Scaling and Growth 178
    Overcoming Adversity 178
    Further Reading 180

Appendix A **183**

Preface

After working at major technology companies for several years designing microchips, in early 2010 I quit my job and joined a four-year-old startup firm as director of engineering. Working at a startup was a unique experience for learning about the dynamics and challenges of a new company. Then, in 2012, I started my own business.

Since then, I have attended numerous workshops, lectures, and networking and entrepreneurship study events in San Francisco and Silicon Valley. Although many of them were very informative, I was struck by how most were insufficient and narrowly focused. At the same time, I immersed myself in reading books and articles about entrepreneurship and learned a great deal. However, the lack of a single book that would give a comprehensive, holistic view was evident.

Along with my firsthand experience, I met numerous enthusiastic entrepreneurs who also were chasing their dreams. I reviewed many business plans and advised people who were starting businesses. Most of them were first-time entrepreneurs who were learning the trials and tribulations of the process. Often, I wished there was a single book that I could recommend to them to read and quickly get up to speed.

This book is the result of my study of entrepreneurship, learning from many masters, working with passionate founders, and advising startup companies. First-time entrepreneurs and those who are in the early stages of building a business should find it useful. However, anyone interested in the topic and those with prior experience will find useful takeaways. I hope reading this book will boost your confidence, accelerate your progress, and help to increase your odds of success. It will be my ultimate reward if you find this a helpful guide for your journey. Congratulations for taking the first step.

Finally, I am grateful to Wolfgang Reißnegger and Katya Falakshahi for reviewing the original draft and providing invaluable feedback. Also, I thank Jeffery Hoffman and William Boughton for professional advice and assistance in polishing the manuscript. My gratitude to Siamak Sartipi for reading the final version and providing useful comments. I wish to thank Daniel Greenberg for masterfully narrating the audio version. This book would not have been possible without the support and encouragement of my family and friends.

Babak Soltanian
San Francisco, California
Fall 2017

Intuitive Entrepreneurship

Introduction

In 2013, I decided to train for a triathlon, an endurance competition consisting of three different sports: swimming, cycling, and running. In a race, triathletes do all three in sequence without a break. The sport has various levels of difficulty, starting with Sprint and going up to Olympic, Half Ironman, and Full Ironman. I signed up for an Olympic-level event, in which athletes swim about a mile in open water, bike for 25 miles, and run for 6.2 miles. I had been biking and swimming since I was a kid. As for running, I'm more of a sprinter than an endurance runner, so my assumption was that running would be my weakest sport.

I signed up for a six-month training course with a Team in Training (TNT) offered by the Leukemia and Lymphoma Society. Every week we had six days of rigorous training and one day off to recover. Experienced coaches taught us techniques and, most importantly, helped prepare us mentally for race day. It was a life-changing experience, and since then I went on to successfully finish five triathlons, plus some other running and biking races. Besides getting into excellent physical shape, I learned many things that one can apply to many other aspects of life. Surprisingly, I found that a triathlete's experience is akin to an entrepreneur's quest to start a successful business. I realized that many lessons learned while training for a triathlon are directly applicable to starting a company.

As I expected, running wasn't my strong suit, and every time we ran I experienced paralyzing pain in my feet after 10 to 15 minutes. For a few weeks, I attributed that to a lack of readiness and kept practicing. But, failing to see any improvement in the situation, I was quite discouraged and finally talked to our running coach about it. I later realized that I should have talked to him sooner. When you recognize a problem, save yourself time and trouble and address it as quickly as possible.

His first reaction was to ask, "Have you fitted your running shoes?" The question was a surprise, and I replied: "What do you mean by fitting?"

"It is imperative to pick the right running shoes and make sure they fit properly. Where did you get your shoes? Did they help you with choosing the right size?" I told him that I had recently bought the shoes from a Nike store and picked them because I liked the design. The sales associate didn't offer to help me with the fitting. The shoes were new, and I had paid top dollar for them.

Following his suggestion, I visited a store called Fleet Feet to have them check my shoes and see if they were the right fit. Right off the bat, the sales associate recommended a larger size. Up to that point, I had been wearing size 10.5, and he said he thought I should wear size 12 to give my feet enough room to expand and still be comfortable. He also recommended a different type of running shoe with a sturdier and more supportive sole. I walked out with a new pair of shoes. On the first practice session with the new shoes, I ran for 30 minutes before feeling any discomfort or pain in my feet. It seemed like magic. The wrong shoes had handicapped me. I was pleased with the outcome, but I still wasn't able to run more than 30 minutes comfortably. With my pace, I still had to run for about one hour to complete the 6.2 miles distance, and I was only halfway there.

Learning from the experience, I scheduled an appointment with a podiatrist to see if anything could be done to help me realize my full potential. The doctor, a triathlete herself, did a thorough evaluation, including taking X-rays. To my surprise, she diagnosed that my arches were collapsing during running and that was the cause of pain in my feet. She recommended a set of shoe inserts that had arch support. Equipped with the new shoes and proper inserts, I managed to run the full length of the race without suffering from any pain.

The lesson here is that it is crucial to have the right tools from the outset. As an entrepreneur, you substantially limit your chances of success if not equipped with the proper and necessary tools. Those can range from your laptop computer to advisors, investors, employees, location, and so forth. Always be mindful and put a premium on acquiring the required skill sets, hiring the best, and using the right tools. This approach is critical to your success.

Starting a business is not easy, but it can be stimulating and rewarding. Usually, it starts with an idea for a new product or service that offers value to prospective customers. It is typical for entrepreneurs to underestimate the challenges or to be zealously overoptimistic. Even serial entrepreneurs sometimes fall into this trap, assuming that previous success guarantees they will succeed in their current venture.

The sheer scope of tasks involved in starting a company can be overwhelming. Founders must juggle many diverse activities while building their enterprise, including designing and developing a new product, financing the operation, building a team, identifying potential customers and markets, legal structure and paperwork, insurance, accounting, and taxes. My goal is to help you gain a strong understanding of the practicalities and nuances of chasing your dream.

Together, we will review the essential elements of starting a business. The idea is to put you on the right track (with the right "shoes") from the beginning and save you a tremendous amount of time and energy. This book offers guidelines and tips about some of the fundamental aspects of starting a business. You may find exceptions to what I recommend here, but it is better not to focus on exceptions as they are rare and usually not repeated.

The book is organized into seven chapters:

In Chapter 1, we get a view of what you are getting into as an entrepreneur. Knowing what it takes is empowering, and prepares you for the journey.

In Chapter 2, I explain the key elements of a robust business plan. No business becomes successful without a solid plan.

After establishing a viable business plan, it is time to learn about structuring and incorporating of business. Chapter 3 covers this.

In Chapter 4, we review different classes of equity and how they are distributed among founders, employees, investors, etc.

In Chapter 5, you learn the art of fundraising and how to approach potential investors.

In Chapter 6, we discuss some practical elements of running a company.

And finally, we close with some insights about "pivoting" and overcoming adversity in Chapter 7.

Intuitive Entrepreneurship

Chapter One

What You Are Getting Into

Having a Realistic Vision

Entrepreneurs have a vision about building a business, and they act on it. They start with a big dream, but know it is wise to start small. Even by entrepreneurial standards, where the sky is the limit, not every big idea is realistic. We should be mindful and not let our dreams go wild. It is important to keep it real. To give an example, like everyone I dread long intercontinental flights. I wonder why there are no supersonic commercial jets in service. Who doesn't want to fly between New York and Paris in two hours instead of eight? Obviously, there is a real pain point to address here, and there should be a very high demand for such a product. Also, technologically it is not an easy task but still feasible. The Concorde, a supersonic airplane built by a joint British and French consortium, flew across the Atlantic for nearly three decades before it was retired in 2003. Concorde was capable of flying at 1,354 miles per hour, compared to today's commercial airliners' top speed of about 600 mph. My dream was to build a business that manufactures commercial supersonic jets, but given my background I never thought of it as a realistic venture for myself. Moreover, the multi-billion-dollar question is whether one can start a business that builds supersonic passenger jets in the first place. Regardless of whether the firm will be profitable, which is critical for a business to survive and grow, the cost of development can be prohibitive. Just to give you an idea, the cost of developing the Boeing 787 reportedly was $32 billion over eight years. In comparison, SpaceX, the aerospace manufacturer and space transport services company, has raised about $1.5 billion so far. You can imagine that just raising capital to build a supersonic jet company is a herculean task.

The point here is to dream big, but be realistic. There are many fascinating product ideas, but you may not stand a chance of making yours a reality. Of course, there are always exceptions, but they usually reach the odds of winning the lottery. As a businessperson, your primary task is to increase the chances of being successful. An entrepreneur has control over this and can make it happen to a large degree. You should always think twice before starting a business while its odds of success are extremely low. Starting a business is not like playing the Powerball.

The Mental Game

People familiar with track and field sports know the distinction between a sprint and marathon. In the former, athletes run as fast as they can for a short period; the latter is a test of endurance. Currently, the world record for 100 meters is 9.58 seconds, set by Usain Bolt in 2009. In contrast, the world record for the marathon is 2:06:32, set by Samuel Wanjiru in 2008. Marathon athletes know that they must pace themselves and not run at maximum speed. The best marathon runners adjust their speed and keep a constant cadence through the race. At the same time, it is critical to stay hydrated and consume sufficient calories during the contest. Runners need to anticipate in advance and take calories, such as energy bars, before they run out of fuel. In addition, they must take enough electrolytes with their water to prevent muscle cramps. Trained marathoners know the importance of planning and executing a hydration/calorie/electrolyte regimen. Otherwise, they may collapse before reaching the finish line.

Other key elements of completing a marathon include patience and mental strength. Many marathoners get tired and feel the pain well before the finish line because it is a very long run. It requires patience and persistence. Despite pain and exhaustion, what carries the athletes through the race and ultimately across the finish line is mental strength. All endurance sports are a mental game, and the outcome is very much affected by the athlete's mental strength.

Starting and running a business is like competing in an endurance sport. As a founder, you need to be prepared and have all the gear and supplies. You must train and prepare yourself. You need to set clear objectives and have a well-crafted execution plan. And when you're ready to hit the road, you must stay patient, keep your pace, and stay mentally healthy. You will certainly face many disappointments and setbacks. The key is to stay focused, keep going, and have patience. Mimicking an endurance athlete is a winning strategy for an entrepreneur, and it makes a tremendous difference.

Having Sufficient Bandwidth

Something I learned the hard way was the limit on my bandwidth and the value of being realistic about time and energy. Bandwidth is a representation of the time and effort one can dedicate to a specific cause or activity. And bandwidth is a limited commodity. We dream of doing things that we love to do. People tend to get excited about a new idea. It is an amazing feeling for those with entrepreneurial spirit to want to jumpstart a business based on an idea for a cool new product. But many falter when it comes to taking the first steps and then executing. The simple reason is that they lack bandwidth and the means to start a business.

I frequently meet people who are in the process of starting a company or are in the middle stages. Most have families, well-paying full-time jobs, and perhaps mortgages. And a good percentage of them want to keep their jobs and start a company on the side. These are people who have an aspiration but who lack the necessary bandwidth.

Here's an example. I knew Kevin for quite some time. He was a scientist working in a research lab. He had come up with an interesting invention that had real potential to improve the diagnosis and prevention of a deadly disease. He enlisted me as his advisor to help start a business based on his invention. We made a list of action items and set up weekly meetings to gauge his progress. We began by making a business plan, and his assignment was to study and prepare its essential elements. My job was to help him fine tune the plan, evaluate the merits of the business, make pitch material, and raise capital. He repeatedly came to our meetings unprepared. It was evident that before meetings he would hastily put together some slides at the last minute. Although I continued coaching and guiding him, it was clear that he was underperforming. I knew that Kevin was a smart and accomplished person, but I also realized he didn't have the bandwidth. Deadlines for papers, project meetings at the lab, and family duties were keeping him fully occupied. I decided to end our meetings. I explained to him that he couldn't make any progress as long as he didn't dedicate sufficient bandwidth to the startup. After some deliberation, he recognized he needed to choose between his demanding, full-time job and starting a company. He decided to stay at his job.

You are setting yourself up for a disappointment if you are not realistic about your bandwidth and what is needed to start a business. To put it simply, keeping a full-time job and starting a company don't go together, and it is a delusion to think otherwise. Of course, you may have heard of exceptions, but my suggestion is not to fool yourself. This doesn't mean you have to quit your job as soon as a new idea strikes. You can do thorough research and planning before launching a business and committing full time. Starting and running a company is very demanding. It requires tremendous mental and physical stamina and dedication. You must be ready for it.

Having Conviction

To outsiders, entrepreneurship looks like a glorious endeavor. People regularly read stories in the media about technology billionaires and their celebrity status. But under the hood, it is a grueling exercise and the chances of success are low—more than 90% of startups fail. To survive and win, you must have agility, strength, skill, connections, the conviction, and of course, some luck.

If you are a first-timer, it is hard to find a good investor to back you up. Nothing is easy, and it takes a lot of energy and time to move forward. You will find it challenging even to get your foot in the door. Your chances are slim if you don't have connections who can recommend you to potential investors. But you may know of, or have heard of, people who seem to have it all sorted out and have a relatively smooth ride. Many professional or serial entrepreneurs have strong networks, and some have already earned their financial freedom through a successful business in the past. But they continue the quest—both for excitement and to multiply their wealth. It is not uncommon to see investors fund the ventures of experienced entrepreneurs and give them big chunks of money relatively quickly. One day you may become one of them, but don't fool yourself into thinking it is going to be smooth sailing.

You have probably heard of or watched the TV singing competition American Idol. Every season, hundreds of thousands of people apply to audition for the show. In cities throughout the United States, applicants line up for hours to sing for the judges as the preliminary test. Ultimately, after several rounds of competition, a handful of finalists vie for the top spot and emerge as the final contenders. The winner, and maybe a few of the runners-up, receive lucrative recording contracts. That represents a successful exit for the winner, but he or she is only one out of hundreds of thousands of competitors. Similarly, many people embark on the journey of starting a business and invest a massive amount of time and effort. But in the end, a very low percentage of them succeed.

Think about it. Are you one of those American Idol applicants who is excited about entering the fray to become wealthy and famous while ignoring the fact that you don't have the voice to be a singer? The point here is to make sure you are not jumping on a fad. If you are sick and tired of your current job or hate your boss, quitting and starting your own company might not be the right course of action, at least not until you have a solid business plan.

You should pursue the entrepreneur's dream only if you strongly believe in your idea and mission. You will hear discouraging comments. Many people, including friends and family, will question your wisdom in founding a startup. Having a firm belief is a powerful drive which can carry you through the difficult times and setbacks. You are unlikely to be successful without it. In this pursuit, you will certainly face numerous challenges and setbacks, and it is impossible to succeed without conviction.

Staying Authentic and Genuine

Occasionally, I meet entrepreneurs who imitate a famous person in their manner of dressing, speaking and so on. I find it annoying when someone is not authentic and genuine. People can easily identify an act and, frankly, an act doesn't make someone more successful or respected. Being yourself is usually perceived as a sign of strength. We should learn from others and adopt their good habits or skills, but there is no need for superficial behavior or looks.

Earning people's trust is a key element of being successful. People base their decision to join your venture on whether they can trust you to deliver. Potential investors must decide if they can trust you with their money and that you can return it with a profit. Potential employees evaluate the opportunity to join a startup based on whether founders and people who run the company make them feel confident about their career growth and a payoff. The same applies to customers, partners, and so on. Therefore, it always pays, at least over the long term, to be authentic and genuine.

Ethics and Principles

Some people think it is acceptable for entrepreneurs to cross ethical boundaries or have a fluid set of principles. I disagree. You don't need an extra headache or unpleasant consequences of compromising on your ethics and principles. Theranos, founded in 2003, raised hundreds of millions of dollars to create a technology to make blood tests cheaper and more convenient for consumers. By 2014, the company's valuation soared to about $10 billion. But, in 2015, The Wall Street Journal and other media raised concerns about its business practices. This exposed the company to multiple investigations by federal agencies and management admitted to wrongdoings. As a result, the valuation collapsed and its founder lost almost all of her multi-billion dollar fortune.

My recommendation is to adhere to a set of principles and be ethically sound from the beginning. There are many examples of people in the business world who stumbled because they ignored this tenet. You should have a clear set of principles and require your employees to follow them as well. This approach puts your enterprise on a solid footing and minimizes the risk of getting into a scandal down the road. Never forget that compromising on principles and ethics is a slippery slope and, at some point, it will catch up with you. A key attribute of highly respected leaders is their integrity, and this is essential for making a company successful.

Some examples of sound business principles and values are equal opportunity, respect for employees and coworkers, fair compensation, openness and collaboration, and intolerance of harassment. Not only should you avoid questionable behavior or actions, but also you shouldn't tolerate those from anyone else. I've read reports of investors using their positions to discriminate or harass entrepreneurs. You should walk away and report the inappropriate behavior to their firm or the authorities. Overall, the best practice is to adhere to business ethics and principles strictly and also not tolerate inappropriate behavior from your investors, customers, or employees. Don't compromise on principles.

Managing Oneself

One of the allures of starting a company is being one's own boss. But it sometimes can create a problem for your productivity and efficiency if you don't play the roles of leader and employee simultaneously. As a leader, you are in charge of setting goals, tracking progress, evaluating and adjusting the course, creating a productive and healthy work environment, and motivating the employees. At the same time, as an employee you should be committed to the plan and execute accordingly. You must be strict about implementing and following the plan. It is easy to become absorbed in operations and forget the leadership part and risk going off course or losing sight of the target. Or you may get so absorbed in the management part and cut yourself unnecessary slack on the execution and deadlines. Striking a balance is crucial, and it is advised to separate the two tasks and set dedicated times for each.

Founders work very hard and for long hours. No doubt what you accomplish has a direct relationship with your efforts if time is spent on the right tasks and is in sync with the business plan. However, this shouldn't be a pretext for ignoring or postponing essential habits. For example, regular physical workouts and taking breaks at the right time are instrumental in staying healthy and sustaining high productivity. In the early days of my career, I often skipped meals or gym workouts because I was so absorbed and focused on work. I accomplished much more than a typical employee but ended up with stomach inflammation, which would have become an ulcer if I hadn't changed my habits. Don't confuse working hard with following an unhealthy lifestyle. You will be much more productive, energetic, and present when maintaining a healthy lifestyle that includes a nutritious diet and regular workouts. Also, giving our brains a periodic break from the main task improves productivity and creativity tremendously.

You should also socialize and spend time with friends and family. Most likely you will have to cut back on those activities, but don't eliminate them entirely. Socialization is conducive to staying sane and grounded. Usually, entrepreneurship is a lonely endeavor and socializing helps keep your spirits high.

Networking

As an entrepreneur, you should engage in networking as an efficient way to know people who may become instrumental to the success of your business. They may become your employees, customers, investors, or mentors. Being resourceful advances your mission and usually makes a difference. It is true that you need to spend a lot of time on product development, especially in the early stages of your startup, but building relationships and knowing people doesn't happen overnight. You need to have a strategy for it and dedicate time and effort to stay connected and expand your network. It is not simply about growing the number of your connections on LinkedIn.

Rather, be selective and target people in your industry and those who have a related background.

You can find a broad range of networking events, especially in cities that have a vibrant entrepreneurial community. Often, alumni events are a prime spot for making connections. Alumni clubs from different schools organize networking events, and you can attend them even if you are not a graduate of their school. Also, some companies and organizations hold events with investors or successful entrepreneurs. Search in your area and find out about such events and try to attend some of them. Moreover, go prepared, have your pitch ready, and know what type of contacts you are looking for at those events. Play the long game, and don't ignore people whom you may not need to call on immediately. I have seen individuals who are looking for capital and therefore only focus on investors to the exclusion of everyone else. They usually miss out on great connections that may come handy in the future, or even right in the present. You would be surprised with how someone's introduction or tips can change the course of your company and push you further towards success.

Outcomes

The ultimate goal of any startup company is to make a successful exit and pay back the investors. An exit changes the trajectory and operation of the enterprise. Usually, shareholders and ownership structure change drastically. Two common and preferable exits are either doing an initial public offering (IPO) or being acquired by another company. In an IPO, the company sells stock to the public by listing shares on a stock exchange. The New York Stock Exchange (NYSE) and Nasdaq are the main exchanges in the United States. Most investors expect an exit sometime down the road. Although continuing the business as a private, standalone company may be profitable, it's not what many investors—especially venture capital firms—consider an acceptable result. So, it is important to keep in mind that you must exit at some point. Like a marathoner, you must either cross the finish line or drop out of the race.

A venture-backed startup either wins by making a successful exit, i.e., its investors are paid back handsomely, or fails by shutting down the operation or selling itself to another company for a loss. Besides winners and losers, some startup companies become zombies. They remain somewhere between growth and a downward spiral. They stay alive by generating lackluster sales or raising more capital from investors. Their growth rate is slow or nonexistent. Sometimes they turn to "dumb money," wealthy entities or individuals who lack the proper skills and knowledge of investing in startups, to buy more time. Often the investors have put in big chunks of money and have a hard time shutting down the company and writing off the investment. These companies offer an opportunity for their founders and employees to have jobs and still hope for a miracle. Usually, the founders' shares are highly diluted and the gig becomes like a typical corporate job—with the benefit of running a business. Becoming a zombie startup is a common outcome and something to avoid.

Intuitive Entrepreneurship

Chapter Two

Business Plan

Proper preparation saves you and others energy and time. Being prepared helps you build credibility with your employees, co-founders, investors, and customers. In this section, we review fundamental features of a robust and viable business plan. Starting a company begins with a product or service idea, but that is just the tip of the iceberg. You must build a case for a business that will grow and profit. Otherwise, it is destined to fail from the beginning.

In this chapter, we review ten essential elements of a sound business plan:

- Product & Technology
- Customer Base
- Customer Acquisition
- Market Size
- Scalability

- Sales Channels
- Competition
- Team
- Unfair Advantage
- Revenue Model

Finally, we discuss prototype and feasibility, budget estimate, corporate social responsibility, and conditions for pulling the trigger and founding a company.

Fundamentals

Product & Technology

In the fall of 2016, my friend Mary called me to set up a get together so that I could hear her new business idea. She wanted me to join her venture as a co-founder. One afternoon we met at a cafe in San Francisco. She told me about her idea for a new method for processing computed tomography (CT) scans. It sounded interesting and seemed useful. But she started to stumble when I began asking questions about product definition. Mary had a novel image-processing algorithm in her mind, but she was not clear about the definition of the final product, nor did she have an outline of how a typical user would interact with and use the product. Oftentimes founders have only an abstract idea and insufficient specifics. Mary and I sat down for several hours and hashed out the product outline and interfaces. A clear product definition helped her to take the first step in building a business plan.

Defining the product and its specification is a necessary step before you start recruiting people or talking to potential investors. Think about how customers would use the product. Is it hardware, or software, or both? Consider essential interfaces. In the above case Mary had to determine how her product would interface with a CT scanner and how users would operate it. You may have an exciting idea, but it is vital to define the product in detail. Make sure you have nailed down the functionalities and key features. Most probably the specs evolve during development, but having a good first draft is essential for the success of your business.

If your product idea is high tech, you need to identify the differentiating elements and what is new and unique about the underlying technology. Depending on the type of technology, you may want to address whether it is patentable and how you can build a high barrier of entry for the competition. We discuss intellectual property (IP) and patents in the next chapter.

Customer Base

A common trap that many tech entrepreneurs fall into is that they have a product in search of customers or that they are solving a problem which doesn't exist. Often, people with a background in science or technology come up with a new product idea, which they think is super cool, but it is a creation in search of a market. The idea suffers from either no serious issue to solve or no available market to address. Sometimes your product solves a problem like widespread access to voice communications; cell phones made telephony ubiquitous. Or it can serve a desire, like Instagram, which offers a platform for sharing pictures. Either way, it is critical to start from a problem or a need that really needs a solution, not the other way around.

Being excited about your product and thinking it is "insanely great," to quote the late Apple founder Steve Jobs, doesn't mean that others have the same view and want to use or pay for it. Many entrepreneurs fall into this common trap. And many stubbornly refuse to accept reality. I have seen this play out over and over. It is essential to determine whether there are potential customers who want the product or service, and that there are ways to monetize that need or desire. Otherwise, your product might be a feature or addition that has no potential for becoming a business. The key is to find out if enough people are going to use or buy your product.

To be grounded and not to drink one's own Kool-Aid, it is paramount to see the product from your target users' point of view. One way to do this is through a good market study early on. You don't necessarily need to hire a market research firm to accomplish this. Instead, I recommend directly contacting your potential customers and hearing their feedback. Preferably you should do this before building a prototype, but sometimes it is hard to gauge enthusiasm before the users see at least an outline. The outcome either validates your vision or gives you an early warning about the viability of the business. Strong enthusiasm for your product is one of the best playing cards when talking to potential investors.

When conducting a market study, you should be all ears and absorb all customer feedback and suggestions. Ask questions to figure out what works for them and what they like to have. Don't skew the results, and make sure you talk to a large, diverse group of customers. I suggest talking to at least several hundred potential customers if it is a consumer product. Don't be shy, and make sure you do a comprehensive study with enough rigor. Have a spreadsheet, and record the key elements of each interview.

Hopefully, you will find enthusiasm for the product. Use customer feedback to fine tune the product definition and the roadmap. Don't lose perspective and get overhyped about the results. One thing to keep in mind is the timeline. Current enthusiasm is a good indicator, but there is no guarantee that it will persist through the time your product hits the market. Be mindful of this fact and make sure you have your finger on the pulse of the market as you move forward. It might be a good idea to refresh market sentiment regularly. You should demand this from your marketing team. And until you hire a marketing expert, that is your job as the founder and CEO of the company. At the end, if your market research indicates a lackluster interest in your product, then you better give the plan additional thought and work. Maybe you should seriously consider shelving it. A brave, realistic, and practical decision saves you a great deal of time and effort.

A term that is often used in entrepreneurial circles is "product-market fit," which means having a good product for a viable market. It doesn't matter that you have a great product idea if there is no market and no one wants to pay for it. The other side of the coin is an existing market and a real need but not having a viable product.

In 2013, I became fascinated by the concept of gene sequencing. The fact that we can sequence the human genome still sounds amazing to me. After studying the gene-sequencing technologies available at the time and how they worked, I had a crude idea for a portable gene-sequencing device. It seemed clear that there was a large market for inexpensive, mobile devices. The argument was that every physician would someday need to have one in his or her office to quickly determine a custom treatment for patients. Aside from the medical aspects, this sounded like a winning product if one could build it. My idea was to create a semiconductor-based product with minimal need for agents and chemistry. After some analysis and speaking with experts, the daunting task seemed to be about the accuracy and reliability. Reaching a repeatable and error-free analysis was imperative. In the end, there was a market, but I didn't have a viable product.

Assume you have a great product idea and can identify potential customers who will buy it. The next question is market size and how scalable the business is. Both are crucial if you are planning to raise venture capital.

Customer Acquisition

Say you have done your research and verified the value proposition and existence of a demand/need for the product.

Then, often entrepreneurs quickly jump into incorporating a company, writing the software code, and talking to investors. But don't rush it. Because there is another essential aspect of the problem, and that is customer acquisition.

Many entrepreneurs overlook this and learn it in a hard way. Smartphone apps are an excellent example of how customer acquisition is a crucial part of the business. Many first-time entrepreneurs come up with exciting ideas for apps. They are pumped up about the value proposition and the competitive landscape. It seems like a perfect idea, and they do a sales analysis and count revenue and profits when they get ten thousand, hundred thousand, one million downloads, and so on. It all looks promising. Then they face the hard, cold reality when they launch their app after spending months on development. The million-dollar question here is not the product itself, but how you are going to stand out among hundreds of thousands of other apps and build and grow a customer base.

I had known Mark since moving to the San Francisco Bay Area in 2006. He had come up with a great idea for a new smartphone app. The idea was to build an intelligent entertainment recommender using machine learning algorithms. The app would adapt to the users' interests and curate a collection of interesting events in their area. He quit his job and coded nonstop for more than six months. Mark even went through the process of registering a company. His beta version became ready and he moved into the customer acquisition phase. It was vital to build a minimum user base to prove the viability of the product. His talks with potential investors weren't bearing any fruit as most of them asked whether he had any users. It was then that he realized how difficult it was to acquire users. Spending a modest amount of money didn't get him very far as the user-acquisition cost turned out to be substantial. Mark ultimately abandoned his venture and took a full-time job at an established technology company. If he had known from the beginning how difficult it is to acquire customers, probably he wouldn't have quit his job in the first place.

Acquiring customers can be cost prohibitive. It is a huge challenge for many startups and one of the main reasons for their failures. One way of doing it these days is to hire college students to sell and market the product to their peers. The downside is the upfront cost that you have to cover. Customer acquisition cost can quickly wipe out any profits that you were expecting. Having a reliable and practical strategy for customer acquisition is critical. However, if there is a huge market to serve and prospects for gigantic revenue, then raising capital to acquire customers and expanding the market share is the right course of action. Many fast-growing startups, like ride sharing companies or online retailers, spend massive amounts of money on customer acquisition and retention.

Market Size

It was a sunny day in Mountain View when I met Jess again after a couple of months. She didn't look very happy. As we sat down for lunch, she pulled a small device out of her purse. It looked like a mechanical valve. In a faint voice, she said it was the killer of her idea: a valve mounted on a shower-head that could stop or open the water flow. It could conserve water when one is shampooing. She was motivated by the severe drought in California and wanted to do something good. I understood her disappointment because she had been working for a few months on an electrical device with solenoid valves and some electronic circuits to control the water flow of a shower head using buttons. At the time, I thought it was a cool idea and something needed. She was very excited about the device and had spent a lot of time on building a prototype. After talking to a good number of potential users and some experienced businesspeople, she realized she didn't have a viable business.

The main arguments against the business were lack of a big enough market and the high cost of educating customers. The cost of water for taking showers is not a big item on a household's monthly expenses in the U.S. So, aside from people who care about conserving natural resources, a high percentage of the population doesn't have the motivation to invest in such a high-tech device. Even those who care may opt for the simple mechanical valve that she had found at a home improvement retailer. Furthermore, it would be hard to find customers in places like the east coast, where water is relatively abundant. Even in her target region, California, agriculture consumes most of the water in the state. Obviously, it was a disappointment for her to see that there was no viable market for her product.

Sometimes there is a product-market fit for our idea, but the market turns out not to be big enough. To make the concept clearer, it is worth looking at the pharmaceutical industry. It is well known that pharma companies spend their R&D dollars on finding cures for diseases that afflict large populations. They usually don't work on drugs for diseases that affect only a small number of people. One of the main factors in deciding what they work on is market size. That is necessary to secure a good return on investment. The same concept applies to startup companies. A good product-market-fit doesn't mean there is a good business if there is not a big enough market.

Of course, market size is a relative concept. Before elaborating, let's look at the definition of a commonly used term in business, total addressable market or total available market (TAM). It refers to the total size of the market for a given product or service. TAM is the number of units sold or total revenue per year. Say for women's handbags, TAM is all the handbags sold around the world in a year. The best way to make sense of what is a good figure for a business to become viable is the ratio of the market size to the capital needed to break even. If you spend more than $1 million to enter a market with $100 million TAM, you should think carefully about going into this business. And for a $20 million TAM, it is probably better not to pursue it, at least not as a venture-backed business. First, a large TAM doesn't mean you are going to capture all of it. Getting 20% of a market is impressive and difficult to achieve. Second, your customer base must be big enough to generate sustainable growth and profit. Otherwise, your investors won't get their money back with a good multiple. However, a market with low TAM might be a great opportunity for building a successful small business.

Jess ultimately stopped working on the product, but there are a couple of other lessons in this case that I would like to point out. First, if she had spent enough time investigating the market before jumping the gun and making the prototype, she would have saved herself a lot of time and energy. Second, a recurring theme in pursuing business opportunities is the concept of "being in the right place at the right time." The world population is growing quickly against the backdrop of limited natural resources and an ever-changing climate. So, there might be a very good market for Jess' product in the not-too-distant future.

Scalability

In 2016, a friend referred a couple of professional baseball players and a baseball enthusiast businessman to me. They wanted us to build a wearable product that would help players perform better by providing them with more accurate statistics. One of the features would be correct reporting of spin data when a pitcher throws a ball. Up to that point, expensive radars that could determine the speed and trajectory of the ball were installed only at major ballparks, and those didn't deliver accurate spin data. Apparently, spin has a profound effect on a pitch, and it was critical for the players to know how they do and how to improve. The radar-based tracking devices were also bulky, and the operators frequently had to fine tune them. We saw a golden opportunity. The pain point and the customer had presented themselves at my doorstep!

We spent a good amount of time defining the product and researching the competition. But I held off on building a prototype. I insisted on doing an analysis of the market and the scalability of the business. To our surprise, we found it was not a scalable opportunity. At best, we could build a robust small business, but it was nothing close to a blockbuster tech startup. In the U.S., only 30 teams play in Major League Baseball (MLB), and the game is not a worldwide phenomenon. Without going into details, this was a case of a great product idea coupled with a proven customer demand, but it failed the scalability test.

An entrepreneur needs to study the scalability of a business adequately. He or she has to look at the possibilities for expanding the business and riding an exponential growth curve. Geographical expansion is a typical way to grow a business. Blue Apron, a meal kit service, started in New York City and then expanded to other big cities. Another way to grow a business is by expanding your target group. Facebook originally started with college students and ultimately opened to everyone. Often the expansion happens in multiple dimensions in parallel or alternatively.

On the other hand, you may find an excellent opportunity to build a small and profitable business. You might be happy with it and not care if it is not very scalable. That is perfectly fine, just don't waste your time and effort chasing venture capitalists. It's unlikely that they will be interested in such a limited opportunity.

Sales Channels

In some industries, controlling sales channels is sometimes more important than the actual product. An entrepreneur may have a great, competitive product, but not having proper sales channels can doom the business. Pharmaceutical is one of those industries where dominant players have an army of sales representatives and control the means of selling a product to potential customers. Competing against those players is a herculean task as they can outperform any new competition by orders of magnitude.

A good example is Mannkind Corporation, a southern California pharma company that invented an easier, less painful method of stabilizing insulin in diabetic patients. Their flagship drug, Afrezza, is an inhalable insulin. Comparing it to the existing alternative—daily or regular injection—reveals its promise. It is hard to argue the case for an injection-based drug versus an inhalable one, and we can see the clear advantage of Afrezza over its competition. That's an excellent example of a perfect product-market fit, and it is reasonable to expect an astounding run for the drug and Mannkind. But to this date, the sales numbers have been quite disappointing. Without going into a detailed account of the story, in summary, this product has failed to capture the potential market because of the company's lack of robust and competitive sales channels. They haven't been able to compete with larger peers in sales prowess and partnerships with insurance companies. The dominant pharma companies enjoy the benefits of massive sales channels and can easily crush any competition from upstarts.

Today, over a billion smartphones are sold every year, and the market is dominated by Apple and Samsung. In mid-2007 Apple introduced its flagship product. The first generation iPhone debuted on AT&T's cellular network, which was the second largest carrier in the U.S. Very soon a serious contender emerged, and it wasn't Samsung, which now enjoys a market share on par with Apple but wasn't even considered a serious competitor back then. The challenger was Palm, Inc. which was a pioneer in successfully bringing Personal Digital Assistants (PDAs) to the market. Palm Pre was much hyped as the iPhone killer and expectations ran extremely high.

Then came time to launch the highly-anticipated product. Many expected to see the new smartphone run on the cellular network of Verizon Wireless, the largest U.S. carrier with even more subscribers and coverage than AT&T. But in 2009 Palm introduced the Pre only on Sprint's network. Sprint was considerably behind AT&T and Verizon in terms of subscribers and coverage. Also, Sprint's reputation was marred by very poor customer support and its finances were not very solid. Sprint couldn't sell enough devices for multiple reasons, including a very poor marketing campaign. Palm botched the sales channel and that was the end of the company. Prospects for success faded quickly and the company's stock plummeted. In 2010, Palm sold itself to HP in a desperation move and one year later HP shut down the operation.

In summary, just having a competitive product and a perfect product-market fit doesn't necessarily translate to success. Controlling the sales channels can be a critical factor as well.

Competition

It is imperative for a startup to thoroughly research its competition. Occasionally I am surprised to hear people talk enthusiastically about their business even though they haven't done even a simple Google search to see who and what they might be up against. Some entrepreneurs confuse two things: we have not seen a product like ours versus there is no such product in the market. You would be surprised how many similar businesses exist which you never heard of before. Often, we haven't heard of a particular product or company because we have not been in the market for that product before. Do not skimp on research on your competition. The result is consequential to your success.

After doing research on the competition, you may face one of the following scenarios:

- There is no such product in the market
- There are many competitors
- There are a few competitors

There is no such product in the market

If this is the case, don't fall into the trap of thinking that nobody has thought of the idea before. It is likely others have already come up with the same idea. One simple reason could be that there is not a big enough market for the product. It might be a great idea and an innovative solution for a real problem, but the total market is small and not attractive. Or it may be that the cost of customer acquisition doesn't leave enough margin to make it a viable business.

Another reason could be technological barriers. The enabling technologies might not be available yet. For example, a paper-thin smartphone may sound like a fantastic idea, but the underlying technologies are not ready yet. You should try to figure out the reasons why there is not already such a product in the market. You should ask why there haven't been any takers yet if there is a pain point and an opportunity to make money. You may find that there have been takers, but they failed. In that case, it is important to know why others failed. It is crucial to learn from their experience. If possible, you should try to speak with them.

If the product is truly innovative and you see a viable business, then you may ride the first mover's advantage and dominate the market before anyone else. But stay curious and try to find out why there is no competition in the first place.

There are many competitors

Usually, this is the case when a new market has recently developed and is still expanding. Success invites competition. You shouldn't have a hard time convincing your potential investors or employees about the market. However, the focus must be on what makes you different from the rest of the pack. In other words, what your competitive advantage is. You also need to have a clear strategy for capturing your target market.

Obviously, you don't have first-mover advantage here, but this can be to your benefit. Sometimes first movers pave the road for the latecomers to reap the rewards with a better product or strategy. Facebook came to the market well after Myspace and Orkut. However, be careful if the competition has already dominated the market. In this case, chances are that the other small players will disappear in a short time. It would be wise to avoid their overconfidence and think twice before joining the hype. A possible opportunity could be replicating dominant players' success in different markets where they are not present. You have a good chance of being acquired or becoming a viable player if your company dominates an underserved market before the leader comes in.

There are a few competitors

This is a plausible situation because it confirms the existence of a market for the product. The market and the product are already proven. Also, that is an affirmation of the feasibility of making the product. However, the challenge is to demonstrate an attractive differentiation concerning existing products. It is usually an uphill battle to take market share from entrenched players. But you may find unaddressed markets that you can cover, such as different geographies. Or your product might have considerable advantages regarding functionality, cost, ease of use, enhanced experience, etc.

You probably have heard of Blue Bottle Coffee. I remember the days when they operated out of a garage in Hayes Valley in San Francisco. I lived in San Jose at the time and most weekends drove up to San Francisco. It was a pleasant ritual to stop at their garage-based store and get a coffee. I liked their product and the experience. In the age of

Starbucks, which has long dominated the coffee market, one might have assumed it was impossible to build a successful coffee chain. But today, Blue Bottle has grown out of its garage and has a presence in major cities like New York, Tokyo, and San Francisco, among others. They raised more than $100 million, and recently Nestle took a 68% stake in the company, which has a valuation north of $700 million. Their differentiation and focus have been on specialty coffee. Customers feel they are walking into an artisan coffee shop, and to some people their coffee tastes better than Starbucks'. The beauty of the business is that the customers happily pay a premium for a cup of coffee at Blue Bottle.

Having few competitors can be a sign of a mature industry. There is a good chance that economy of scale is the only game in the industry. These markets usually offer low margins. Or it could be the product is very complex, requiring large investments in R&D and mass production. As a rule of thumb, big R&D investments and small margins are red flags for investors. Big prior investments just to develop and bring a product to the market present a high risk that many investors don't want to take. The likelihood of success for a startup is not high when economies of scale and small margins are at play in its target industry. In the fundraising chapter (Chapter 5), we discuss investor motives and goals in more detail.

Another thing to be aware of is consolidation in your industry, as it makes starting a new business a daunting task. The semiconductor or microchip industry is one of the latest to go through large-scale consolidation. In the late 1990s, there was a boom in the number of startup chip makers riding the wave of wireless technologies and the Internet. Many newcomers took chances on bringing new technologies to the market. Ultimately, however, a handful of big players emerged. The industry went through a massive consolidation starting around 2015, and this trend continues.

If there are a few competitors in your target market, you should focus on differentiation and work to surmount the barriers of entry built by your competition.

Team

Assume your idea checks against all the key elements of a successful business plan that we discussed so far. Then the next step is assembling a team of professionals who can execute the plan and bring the business to life. Without a competent team, everything else is just words on paper. The team is so critical that by itself it can make or break a startup business. One of the top items for savvy investors considering funding your company is the caliber of your team. Never talk to investors or pursue the business if you don't have the required talent on board, and it's better not to settle for mediocre or underperforming staff because that will hamper your progress.

A question that I often hear from first-time entrepreneurs is whether they need to have at least one co-founder to be able to raise money. If you have assembled a strong, quality team, then it matters less whether you have a co-founder or not. The key is to have the right people to make the product and build a business. For the sake of redundancy, some investors may prefer two or more co-founders, but it is not an absolute necessity to have co-founders. Many successful startups have only one founder. So, if the business plan is solid, a strong team is assembled, and you have covered all the important aspects of the firm, then you are ready to go.

However, don't ignore the value that a good co-founder can bring to the business. I recommend you search for the right match, someone who has complementary skills sets and shares your passion for pursuing the dream. Besides, many times you will find yourself lonely and stressed out while building a business. Balancing the load and having someone to back you is priceless. Make sure you are not dismissing potential co-founders just because of greed and wanting to keep most of the equity to yourself. Keep in mind, the value of a company is like a pie. Having a smaller slice of a very large pie is worth much more than having all of a minuscule pie. Building a company is about increasing the size of the pie and it can't be done without sharing it.

As a rule of thumb, it is better to have one or more very good co-founders, but not too many. Spend some time finding the right person and signing them up. I recommend someone whom you have worked with before and know that you two are going to get along well. If you and your potential co-founder haven't worked together before, then you should be more cautious about finding the right person. Consider going solo as the last option if there is no one to bring onboard.

Friends and Family

In the fall of 2004, I took my first course at Columbia Business School. It was about business fundamentals. In one session, the professor described the pitfalls of bringing friends and/or family into your business. He strongly advised against it. My experience proved his point, and I recommend not going into business with friends and relatives.

It is typical for entrepreneurs to start a business with friends or family. They talk about the idea and get excited about the prospect of the venture. Surprisingly, the first people we recruit as co-founders or key employees are often our friends and family. It is natural to start with people you know well and trust. But in selecting employees, you must always think about their skill sets and how well you know their work. Next, it is important to have a work history or not, especially for key positions and co-founders. You may be close friends and admire each other's accomplishments, but you do not have any experience working together. A lack of previous work cooperation is potentially a problem, because the parties may have different styles and might not be able to form a productive working relationship. Being close friends or family does not necessarily mean you can work well together. The message is to think twice before partnering with a friend or a relative.

Unfair Advantage

Unfair advantage is a phrase that is frequently tossed around by investors and entrepreneurs. In this context "unfair" means one-sided or uneven, and not unjust or against principles. The words simply refer to what makes a business capable of capturing a big share of a market. To build a viable business, you must have an edge on the competition. That is the only way you can dominate a market and grow the business. Otherwise, trying to unseat entrenched competitors is going to be an uphill battle, and probably a lost cause. The advantage doesn't necessarily have to be about the product, but can be things like having a robust sales channel, a considerably lower cost to the customer, a premium service or product, support for multiple platforms, the number of users, or the management team. It is called unfair advantage because your competition has a hard time copying your position. It is crucial to identify your unfair advantage and be able to explain why you have it.

At the time of writing, I am serving as an advisor to a medical software startup. The firm is developing a novel method to provide insights and information about a patient's heart. The data can potentially save many heart patients or help others prevent heart attacks in the future. The idea and the mission are phenomenal. In a long session with the entrepreneur, we tried to identify his unfair advantage. It happens to simply be the team's knowledge and the company's innovation, a new method to process medical images. No one else has this advantage, and it is not easy to copy quickly.

Revenue Model & Margins

The ultimate goal of a business is to make profits, maybe not in the short term but definitely in the long run. You need to sell your product or service to make money. Therefore, it is crucial to be clear about how that is going to happen from the beginning. A proper revenue model strongly depends on the type of service or product, no matter whether you are a business-to-business (B2B) or business-to-consumer (B2C) company.

In an advertising model, customers receive the service for free and the company generates revenue from selling advertisements, as is the case with Facebook or Google. Or the firm could sell products and services for a particular price, such as Apple, Oracle, Microsoft, American Airlines, and Hugo Boss. Another approach is the "freemium" model where the enterprise offers a bare-bones service or software for free and charges a premium for the full version. Evernote, which makes an app for note taking, organizing, and archiving, is an excellent example of this model. Also, there is the subscription model in which you earn money by selling monthly subscriptions—Netflix and Hulu employ this framework. Some companies have developed a hybrid model. For example, Amazon both sells products directly to customers and offers subscription services.

You should carefully define which model works best for your product. Having a hybrid and complex model in the beginning may not be a reasonable approach for a startup company. The combination of the revenue model, anticipated market size, and estimated market share can give you valuable insight into the expected revenue.

Finally, you must have an estimate of an acceptable price for your product. Naturally, the next question is how much it is going to cost you to make it. The difference between sales price and the cost of manufacturing or developing is called gross margin. Usually the margin is expressed in percentage of the final cost. A 60% gross margin means the cost of the product to you was 40% of the sales price. Higher margin leaves you more money from each sale, which generally translates to a higher profit. You should be very careful about estimating your sales price and margins. The shelf price is not your sales price if you're planning to sell through retail channels. For example, if the price tag for your product in a store is $100 and the cost of making it is $50, you might be surprised to find that you don't have a viable business. When selling through retail, the total cost of the product ought to be about one-fifth of the shelf price to make your business profitable. Otherwise, your company will struggle to survive.

Prototype & Feasibility

It is a smart move to build a prototype when your business plan is sound and has merits. Nothing has a more powerful impact on potential investors or customers than showing them a sample or a prototype. First, they can play with it and see how the product looks in real life. Second, it gives you credibility, as it demonstrates your team's skills and capabilities. It shows that you can do it. Never underestimate the power of a real prototype. But keep in mind that if done poorly, it will seriously undermine your credibility and potential. Making a robust prototype for a reasonable amount of investment and effort is an art form. It doesn't need to be perfect, but it should leave the target audience with a good impression.

Budget Estimate

Funding your startup is the next logical step after verifying that you have a sound business plan. Typically, you raise several rounds of capital to build the product and grow the business before exiting. It starts with the "seed" round, followed by rounds A, B and so forth. Each time you raise capital, you exchange equity in your company for money. There is always a tradeoff between how much you raise and how much dilution you accept. As an entrepreneur, you must be vigilant and smart about this. It is important to raise the right amounts at the right times. Not raising enough money will starve your business and put it at a significant risk. Raising too much shows a lack of discipline and usually comes at a steep price concerning dilution.

Keep in mind that raising capital usually takes a lot of time and energy. It can go on for months, depending on how many investors you bring in and who your investors are. It is an involved process, and typically you end up talking to many investors before closing a deal. Take all this into consideration regarding your timeline.

Before contacting any potential investor, you need to answer three fundamental questions:

- What goals or milestones are you planning to achieve with the funds?
- How long is it going to take to accomplish those goals?
- How much money do you need?

First, determine what the goals and milestones are that you are planning to achieve with a round of funding. Be accurate and clear. It is not sufficient to just list items like hiring three engineers or building a beta version of an app. Specify what type of expertise you are recruiting and approximately when they are coming on board. Have an estimate of their compensation. Also, have sufficient details about the beta version, if that is the goal.

Second, identify how long it will take your team to accomplish those objectives. For tech startups, it typically takes from six to 18 months from building a prototype to releasing a beta version. Raising money for a short runway and then going back to raise more is a bad strategy.

Third, you need to know how much money you need to achieve your goals for this round. Make a spreadsheet and list all expenses for running the business during this period. Some of the main items are staff, office space, furniture, tools, utilities. Try to make a complete list and don't leave out anything of significance. Adding a reasonable budget for rewarding your staff occasionally is not a bad idea. And being frugal is highly advised. At the same time, be careful not to create a harsh and unproductive work environment. I advise you to seek help if you don't have prior experience with budgeting and estimating the costs of starting a business.

A question that entrepreneurs often ask is how much money they should raise. The answer is straightforward: raise the amount you need, nothing more, nothing less. And you should quickly come up with the number if you carefully follow the previous steps and determine the goals, time you need to make it happen, and what it takes to get there.

Now that you have the base estimates of the cost and the duration of a phase of your business, you need to adjust and make them more practical. It is likely that you have underestimated the numbers. You should increase those estimates by, say, 25%. Otherwise, you may face budget overruns or slack in the execution. For example, R&D usually takes more time and effort than original estimates. Coming up short before reaching a major milestone puts your business at significant risk. You may run out of money before being able to have a new cash infusion. Also, raising money in such a situation comes at a steep price because you haven't eliminated any significant risk by achieving a milestone yet, and the valuation is not going to be attractive.

Corporate Social Responsibility

For a long time the sole mission of a corporation was touted to be maximizing shareholders' returns. This is still the main purpose of any for-profit business. But, these days, a new trend has gained traction and that is social responsibility. Nowadays, thoughtful entrepreneurs and businessmen are setting Corporate Social Responsibility (CSR) as one of their business values. They take a more conscientious approach to all the stakeholders and advocate wellbeing of their employees, communities, environment, and so forth. Sustainability and further reliance on renewable energies are among their top goals. In this new value model, a corporation assumes an active role in implementing some social good and serving a higher purpose alongside making a profit. Some corporations give back a percentage of their profits to the communities in need, or commit to developing environmental friendly products and reducing their polluting byproducts. A good avenue for a business to be a force for good is to become a Certified B Corporation (B Corp). The certificate verifies that a firm meets the highest standards of social and environmental performance, public transparency, and legal accountability. I am a strong believer in CSR and think as a visionary and forward looking entrepreneur you should commit to this principle from day one. It is easier to build a business on these values from early days rather than changing course later.

Pulling the Trigger

I hope you realize by now that there is much more to having a solid business plan than just a great product idea. We looked at the fundamentals and how each element plays a vital role. The product must offer a tangible value to potential consumers. You may have sound instincts about some of the fundamentals that we already discussed, based on years of experience, but going through a rigorous process of studying and addressing all these items pays off handsomely. Going through this exercise at the outset saves you from frustration and wasting a lot of time and money later. Certainly, there are myths about people who drew a product idea on the back of a napkin and were able to raise capital for it. Those are folks with exceptional track records in building companies, and they are very rare. You can certainly raise money even without a drawing on the back of a napkin if you are already in the league of Bill Gates, Elon Musk, or Jeff Bezos. Otherwise, it is better to go through all the steps and address all the essential elements of a business plan before approaching anyone for money.

We learned that there are many dimensions to crafting a viable business plan. After going through all the steps and addressing the business from different angles, it is not uncommon for entrepreneurs to face an unclear situation and be unsure about how to proceed. They may realize that some aspects of the plan are superb, and some are not that promising. You are at a fork in the road, one direction leads to pulling the trigger and vigorously pursuing the business, and the other leads to abandoning it all together. Qualitative aspects sometimes make things ambiguous. To make things a little easier, Figure 1 walks you through major steps in your decisions about how to proceed.

The key here is to know which elements are must-haves and which ones can be fixed or acquired. Having a viable product-market fit, a sizable market, a competent team, and an unfair advantage are must haves. The rest might be fixable.

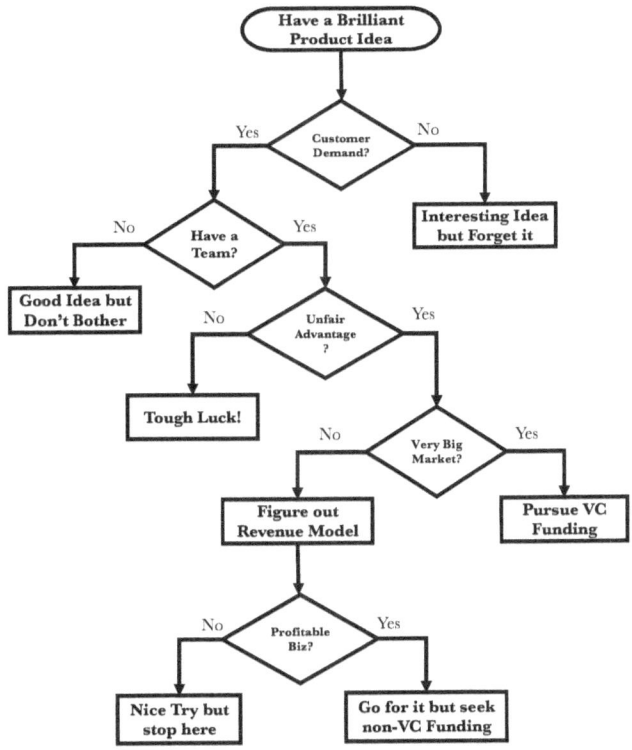

Fig. 1 – Decision flow chart on starting a business

Chapter Three

Structure

Legal Considerations

Invariably, you will have to deal with a host of legal issues while forming and running a company. Those start with incorporating the business, and expand to include employment, stock options, raising capital, contracts with customers or suppliers, etc. These days you can do some of the legal paperwork yourself or through online services, which usually cost less than an attorney. However, hiring a good lawyer can make your life much easier and let you focus on the main tasks at hand. The requirements are a complex web of Federal, state, and city laws, and it is impossible for you to know and manage all of that. Besides, to be a successful entrepreneur you need to know how and when to delegate. Please budget for legal fees and include that in your estimates. If you are cash strapped and can't afford to hire a lawyer, there are ways to pay less for legal advice. For example, some lawyers do pro bono work. In the end, it is worth having an attorney who can advise you whenever necessary. Legal mistakes take more time and money to fix after the fact.

Inexperienced entrepreneurs may quickly add legal issues to their growing list of challenges. It usually happens because of ignorance or lack of funds to hire a lawyer. It is possible to take missteps in either or all these phases: incorporation, employment, intellectual property, and raising money.

Some typical mistakes regarding incorporation are the type of company structure you choose, the jurisdiction the company is incorporated in, and how you limit your liabilities. Another mistake is to sacrifice the structure most suitable in the long term for temporary benefits in the short run. For example, assume you are based in California and want to raise venture capital sometime down the road. The right choice could be a C-Corp incorporated in Delaware but operating in California. But you may instead settle on an S-Corp incorporated in California to limit some of the expenses and benefit from a pass-through tax structure. You will learn more about these structures in the next section.

Another typical example is the way founders split their shares or ignore putting a vesting period in place.

Another issue that can cost you a lot and affect your business is the ownership of intellectual property (IP). It is important to identify who the inventor is and who owns the patent. A typical situation that I have seen is with people who are planning to start a business based on inventions and IP developed while the founders were working at a university or research institute. The outcome of their research might be in the public domain, and the institute may not have any claim on it. However, the institute may have some claim on the results of your job. If you are in such a situation, I recommend consulting with a patent lawyer to determine the right course of action. Also, you may consult with the proper office at the school to see how you can use the results. It is likely that you will have to license the technology or inventions from the university and pay them a royalty on a commercial product. Also, you should be mindful of any claims to your IP from other people who have contributed to the invention, like former employees or collaborators. Or, if the IP belongs to you or a company's employee, you need to transfer the IP to the enterprise and do it officially and legally. Similar concerns apply to copyrighted material as well.

Employment is another aspect that you should be careful to put in the right legal framework. You have to make sure your company follows all applicable Federal, state, and local employment laws. It is always preferable to have a signed contract with anyone working at the company in any capacity. Basic items to include in the contract are the scope of responsibility, compensation, a clause about work at will, a non-disclosure agreement (NDA), and an IP assignment agreement. Also, it is important to determine the jurisdiction for any legal disputes. Without going into details, it makes a difference if the jurisdiction is the state of New York or California. Another matter that you need to pay attention to is the Federal, state, local, unemployment, and other taxes that you must withhold from the employee or pay as an employer. Moreover, the structure of equity compensation is something to craft carefully. And you'd better apply all these items to founders as well, and treat them as employees of the company.

Please note that the material covered in this book is not a substitute for professional legal advice. The goal is to give you some ideas about the complex issues that you may face and how important it is to seek help from a lawyer. Another example is that there are some securities laws that founders and employees must adhere to and file proper forms on time. Not knowing about them is not an excuse, and it may cost you later to fix a simple mistake. Acting based only on short-term benefits can catch up with you in the future and cause extra headaches and expenses. It may delay your progress and completely wipe out any benefits that you have already gained from the original setting. So, it is advisable to start with the right legal structure from the beginning to keep your enterprise on the right track.

Legal Entities

What type of incorporation to choose is usually confusing, especially for first-time entrepreneurs. There are different types of legal forms, and most likely one of them is best for your venture. The type of corporation has an enormous impact on raising money from potential investors, granting equity to employees, tax liabilities, and has legal ramifications. Although it is possible to change the legal form down the road, that is costly and burdensome. Moreover, not selecting the right framework is a recipe for headaches and extra paperwork. Therefore, it pays to be careful in selecting a proper legal structure. There are six legal structures for operating a for-profit entity:

- Corporation (C-Corp)

- S Corporation (S-Corp)

- Limited Liability Company (LLC)

- Partnership

- Sole Proprietorship

- Cooperative (Co-op)

This section provides a global view of how to choose the proper format without delving too much into the details. The goal is to give you the basic idea about each structure and ultimately put you on the right path to figuring out which form fits the best with your business. For accurate and comprehensive advice, you need to consult with a lawyer who practices corporate law. Choosing the right business entity depends on different parameters. My goal here is only to present you with some tips and decision-making factors when you arrive at the point of formally structuring your business.

C Corporation

Let's start with Corporation, or what is usually called C-Corporation or C-corp. A corporation provides a legal framework to issue shares in exchange for capital, and also protects shareholders with limited liability. If you are planning to raise venture capital (VC) money, then this should be your choice. Because of favorable legal frameworks and tax laws, most VCs want you to incorporate in the state of Delaware, regardless of the location of your headquarters. Also, a C-Corp is an appropriate structure for granting stock to employees and advisors. It is an entirely independent entity and has all the means to grow the business, raise capital, and expand the shareholder base.

Please keep in mind that the company still has tax and legal liabilities wherever it operates, even if incorporated in Delaware. Incorporating in a state other than where your base is located adds extra overhead and expenses. The corporation pays taxes on its income independent of your income or the salary you are paying yourself. In certain cases, this might result in paying extra taxes compared to other legal structures.

S Corporation

Legally, an S Corporation (S-Corp) is not very much different from a C-Corp, but there are a few important differences. The main differences are how owners and the company pay taxes and the equity structure. Unlike a C-Corp, you are taxed at the personal level when running an S-Corp. An S-Corp is a pass-through entity, which means profits and losses can pass through to the shareholders' tax returns; consequently, the S Corporation is not taxed directly. To clarify this, let's look at a simple example. Say you fully own a C-Corp and you also are on the payroll as an employee. Assume the company makes $100,000 in total revenue and $20,000 in net income over a year, and you paid yourself $50,000 out of the $100,000 revenue as your annual salary. At the end of the year, you must file your personal tax returns and report $50,000 of income from the form W2. You pay taxes on this income after deductions, and that is independent of the C-Corp's tax returns. Then the C-Corp must file corporate tax returns and pay taxes on $20,000 of profit. If the company ends up with a net loss of, say, $10,000, then you report that on the tax returns. In either case, it does not affect your personal tax liability.

If the same company is incorporated as an S-Corp and you are the sole owner, then the $20,000 profit (or $10,000 loss) appears directly on your personal tax returns as income (or loss). This income is in addition to the $50,000 salary. In this case, the base for your income on the personal tax return is $70,000 (or $40,000). In other words, the profit or loss of the S-Corp is lumped in with your personal income and is taxed. It does not matter if you take the money or leave it in the company—you are still liable to report and pay taxes on the profit. In contrast, the business and individual taxes stay independent from each other in a C-Corp.

It might be disadvantageous to operate as an S-Corp if you are in a high tax bracket, because business tax rates could be lower. Also, it is important to understand that the income is divided between the shareholders solely based on their ownership percentage, regardless of how long each of them has worked in the company. Furthermore, if you want to keep the money in the enterprise without being personally taxed, then a C-Corp should be your choice as an S-Corp doesn't offer this flexibility. Again, this is a simple scenario, and I strongly recommend consulting a Certified Public Accountant (CPA).

Another significant difference between an S-Corp and a C-Corp is equity structure and flexibility. S-Corps can only issue one class of shares, and the number of shareholders is limited to 100. Having only one class of shares does not mean that you cannot have voting and non-voting shares in an S-Corp. C-Corps have the most flexibility for raising capital, issuing different classes of stock, and expanding the equity structure. As soon as you raise VC money, the company must issue both preferred and common shares, and that is only possible under a C-Corp structure. Also, it is typical to have more than 100 shareholders in a growing startup company. Regardless of the tax implications, just the possibility of issuing a different class of stocks and being able to expand the number of shareholders can be determining factors in the structure of your business. It is not very complicated to convert an S-Corp to a C-Corp if the need arises.

Limited Liability Company

As is evident from the name, a Limited Liability Company (LLC) provides limited liability similar to corporations. An LLC offers a different kind of flexibility, and it is easier to manage in terms of paperwork and compliance compared to corporations. Instead of shareholders, LLC owners are called members, who can be one or more people, or other corporations and LLCs.

Like an S-Corp, an LLC is a pass-through entity regarding tax liabilities, and the owners are liable for taxes on the profits whether the money is retained by the company or distributed. However, in an LLC, shareholders (members) have more flexibility in assigning what percentage of the profit is distributed to each member aside from their ownership percentage. For example, if the company has two owners and each of them owns 50% of the business, you can still divide the profits and losses between them in a 75% to 25% ratio, where each one is only responsible for the taxes on their respective portions. In other words, profits and losses in an LLC can be divided among the owners in any ratios regardless of their ownership stake. LLCs can also have different classes of membership. Like an S-Corp, an LLC is not necessarily the right vehicle for raising venture money. Also, it is more challenging and costly to convert an LLC to a C-Corp if you start as an LLC and decide to raise funds down the road.

Partnership

A partnership is a kind of business entity which has two or more owners. There are different types of partnerships with a variety of scopes and responsibilities, but one main difference between a partnership and other forms of business, such as an S-Corp or LLC, is the issue of liabilities. Each partner has personal liability for the debt of the partnership, and they are legally responsible for the actions of other partners. A partnership is not a common type for startup companies, so I recommend that interested entrepreneurs to do more research on this kind of business if they have good reasons for considering it.

Sole Proprietorship

A sole Proprietorship is a simple and barebones type of business that has only one owner who is responsible for all the actions and debts of the company. At the same time, he or she can collect all the profits. A sole proprietorship is a good structure for freelancers. It is an unincorporated type of business, and an individual acquires the status based only on his or her business activities. Still, you need to obtain appropriate licenses and permits. Regulations vary depending on the state and city in which you are operating, so make sure you are familiar with all the requirements. If you decide to operate under a business name, then you need to register the chosen name with your city.

One thing to consider regarding sole proprietorship is legal protection. Generally, when you operate in the framework of a company (S-Corp, C-Corp, or LLC), your personal assets are not at risk in the event the business goes bankrupt or faces legal challenges. But a sole proprietorship doesn't offer that level of protection.

Cooperative

Cooperative (or co-op) is simply a user-owned entity where those who use its products and services operate and control the organization. Typically, a co-op distributes profits among its members. To be more precise, and according to the International Cooperative Alliance, a cooperative is an autonomous association of persons united voluntarily to meet common economic, social, and cultural needs and aspirations through a jointly-owned and democratically controlled enterprise. For example, Recreational Equipment Inc. (REI) is a famous U.S. retail sporting-goods co-op which is owned by its members. The company has more than six million members, and they all receive a dividend which can be used for future purchases. Also, REI members can vote in selecting the board of directors. Other examples are cooperative banks. Choosing a co-op as the legal form for a startup company is not common, but it might be the right framework in rare occasions.

Incorporation Flow Chart

Figure 2 is a flowchart that makes it easy to decide what legal form is the right choice. I advise you to use this chart as the starting point. After finding the proper structure, you should study the nuances of the legal entity to make sure it is the correct choice. It is also a good idea to consult with a professional to verify your selection.

Structure

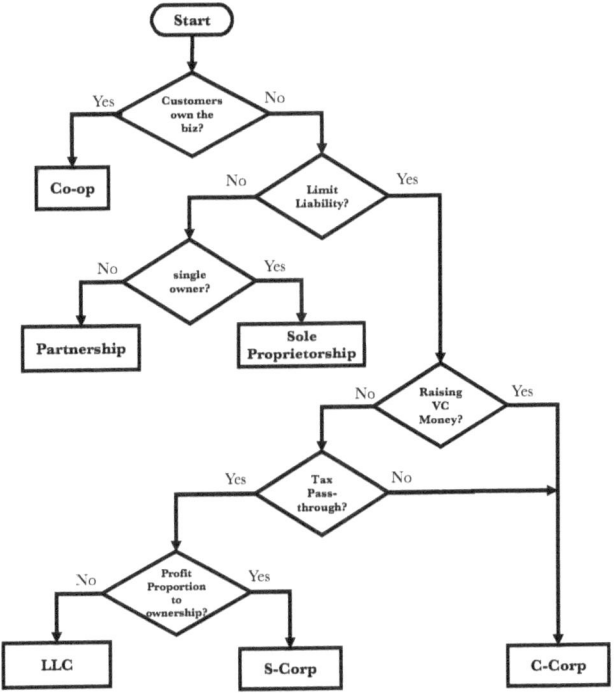

Fig. 2: Selecting proper legal entity for a startup company

Board of Directors

All companies, including startups, must have a board of directors which is responsible for making important, high-level decisions. The board hires a CEO and determines compensation, has a say in hiring top officers, votes on fundraising, decides on a potential exit, and sets the general direction of the company. You need to have a board of directors, even if you are the founder and the only person working in the enterprise. In the beginning, the board can be only one person, but the board will need to expand as the company grows. A thriving startup is likely to bring on a new board member after each round of fundraising.

Founders have full control over the company and its direction. But adding new members to the board usually reduces that power. When you raise money, investors ask for seats on the board to exert their influence. Aside from rare exceptions, at some point entrepreneurs lose control and investors have the final say. A board which is controlled by investors can even decide to replace the founder CEO. Or they may vote to change the direction of the company. There are a few exceptions, like Google or Facebook, where the founding entrepreneurs kept their voting majority in the company—not to be confused with ownership percentage. In those cases, the founders gave away ownership in the firm as they raised money from investors, but they maintained their influence on the board of directors by holding the right to a majority vote. Unless you are in a similar position and have a transformative product and a massive market, the chance of having the right to a majority vote is slim to none.

If you are a founder CEO, it's best not to be obsessed with control and accept the fact that you have to work with the board. What is important is to build a productive working relationship with your board and deliver on progress and milestones. Also, you and the company can tremendously benefit from their service, because presumably they are experienced professionals who are committed to helping the company succeed. The key is to make sure the board is composed of top-notch people who can add a lot of value. People not familiar with your industry or not dedicating enough time can be a drag; you must keep high standards and insist on having board members who can add value to the company. Moreover, make sure you have independent members on the board, people who are veterans of the industry or highly accomplished people. Again, the measure should be their contribution and the value they add to the company.

Patents & Intellectual Property

Intellectual property (IP) is one of the interesting conversation topics that I usually have with entrepreneurs. Most of them think it is simple and straightforward: you have an excellent idea to start with—it is subjective what makes an idea great from the business point of view—and file a patent application, raise money, and ultimately block every competitor. In reality, there is much more to it than that. There is a misconception among inexperienced entrepreneurs that their chances of raising money are much higher when they have issued or pending patents. I have seen entrepreneurs spend thousands of dollars on legal fees to file a patent, a process that they ultimately find utterly useless. If your motivation for filing a patent application is to raise money, then just stop there and put it aside. Robust and viable business plans get funded—not patents. Your only reason for filing for a patent is when you have a unique technology or solution and there is a real possibility of infringement by competitors. Patents only come into play in the technology/product and unfair advantage part of a business plan where you need to explain if they fall into the category of solutions that can be protected by patents. You also want to know how competition might react to your product and whether you can build a barrier to entry. Good counter-examples are all kinds of shared-economy businesses like Airbnb and Lyft. We all know many successful businesses built on those ideas. Almost none of those shared-economy products are patentable, so rivals can easily copy them. Thinking of filing a patent for those kinds of activities is more like a joke, but at the same time, we see multi-billion-dollar companies thrive on non-patentable ideas. Even in industries where patents matter, such as semiconductors or microchips, it is an extensive portfolio of patents that protects the business and creates a substantial barrier to the entry. A single or a few patents won't take you very far. Usually high-tech companies defend their turf with strong patent portfolios.

I often see people who have an interesting idea get carried away and want to file a patent application. Unfortunately, it is not that simple. First, not every idea is patentable. Generally, it is tough to obtain a patent on software. Even if you get the patent, it may prove to be useless. The story with hardware is different, and it is easier to get patents on innovations in this category. However, having a patentable idea still doesn't mean you should rush to apply with the United States Patent and Trademark Office (USPTO). The right way to approach this is to justify why you need a patent and how it is going to help with the business. Also, it is useful to speak with a patent attorney, even for a provisional application, because the language and descriptions define the exact scope and reach of the IP. Also, you don't want to leave room for possible workarounds or alternative variations. I suggest you begin by writing up a one-page justification and list pros and cons of filing for a patent. Moreover, list or briefly describe the merits and avoid verbose descriptions or marketing claims.

Say you have a great product idea and believe you must protect it with a patent. Assume you have done your homework and made sure it is a patentable idea. The next step is to determine what operational leverage it gives the business if granted. Or, a better approach is to start with working out a strategy for building a strong barrier of entry. You may need to innovate further and file more patent applications to make the wall high and impenetrable. Even in those cases, some competitors may infringe your IP and copy it. Having patents is not a foolproof deterrent, but they do give you the upper hand in any legal battle. Some competitors may risk infringing others' IPs to gain market dominance or benefit from first-mover advantage. Despite knowing you own the IP, they may make such a move based on your lack of financial power to sue a competitor and engage in a legal battle. You'd then spend tons of money before getting any results. By the time you bring them to the court, they may have dominated the market. In the end, a larger competitor probably will settle by paying compensation if you are tenacious and lucky enough. That is why your first order of business must be dominating the market as soon as possible. The opportunity can easily slip through your hands if you become comfortable with the false sense of security based on patents, either pending or granted. In the U.S., "patent pending" only serves as a warning to competitors that they may be liable if they infringe on the invention, but it does not have any legal effect. You only have the rights to the invention when the actual patent is issued.

To reduce legal costs and get priority regarding timing, some entrepreneurs file provisional applications. The patent office doesn't look at a provisional application, it is only a time stamp giving you priority in case someone else files for the same innovation. From the date of filing a provisional, you have one year to file the patent application, and the provisional application will serve as the basis of your innovation and priority. So, it is also important to make sure the provisional is comprehensive enough and covers all aspects and variations on the idea. Again, it is a good idea to have a patent lawyer who knows your field to help with drafting the provisional application.

Keep in mind that the USPTO's evaluation process is lengthy. If the patent office doesn't ask for further information and everything goes smoothly, it can take a few years to have the patent approved and granted. If you want to protect your idea in other countries and receive international protection, that adds another layer of cost. There is not a single entity to file an application with and get protection across the globe. Every country has its own laws and procedures for evaluating and granting patents. You should be careful and strategic about filing a patent application in other nations. Choosing more countries means much more cost, time, and effort. Typically, you should submit applications in a handful of countries at most. Those are the countries that host your potential competitors.

To summarize, a patent grants the owner rights to make, use, or sell the product or idea and excludes others from doing so. But no one can patent public-domain knowledge and ideas. There are two types of patents: Utility and Design. Utility patents are about how an idea or invention works. Utility patents are valid for 20 years, and after this period they become public, at which time anybody can use them. Design patents are about what a product looks like, and they are valid for 15 years if filed on or after May 13, 2015.

Oftentimes companies resort to keeping their ideas and inventions as trade secrets rather than filing for patent protection. When you file a patent application, the information and details of the product become public, and it exposes your business to workarounds and even infringements. It is not an easy task to enforce protection of your IP, and it is usually costly and takes a long time. So, many competitors benefit from this and capitalize on your limitations in litigating an infringement. Often it makes more sense to keep the IP as a trade secret and not give any clues by filing a patent application. Many companies monitor patent applications to know about new products and what their competitors are doing. Deciding between filing a patent application or keeping the idea as a trade secret is a delicate matter. One useful indicator is the possibility of reverse engineering your product and learning about its core IP. If that is a possibility, then you should assume the competitors are going to reverse engineer your product and file a patent application that will block you and others. So, you'd better file for a patent if your product can easily be reverse engineered.

Finally, make sure the company owns the IP. Have everyone working for the company (founders, employees, advisors, contractors, board members) sign a non-disclosure agreement (NDA). Also, you need to have a clause in their contract that they assign anything they develop to the company.

Organization Chart

Some entrepreneurs spend substantial time and energy on assigning positions and titles to team members. As a rule of thumb, it is better to make assignments based on responsibilities and avoid grandiose titles. For example, instead of vice president of cloud services, you can just say lead of cloud services. This approach is practical and most importantly gives you room and flexibility to grow. Also, you avoid lengthy and involved discussions about titles and so on. Keep it straightforward and real. As long as your firm is a small team, the best practice is to have a flat organization and titles based on responsibilities and functions.

Chapter Four
Equity Dilemmas

The market value of a business is like a pie which grows in size as you build the business. Your goal is to enlarge the pie and along the way share it with people who help you build the business. Successful entrepreneurs bring a wide array of contributors, including investors, engineers, sales associates, etc. to the business and they know sharing the pie is part of the game. You essentially trade equity in exchange for commitment and contribution from co-founders and employees, and capital from investors. There is not a single formula for this exchange and the rate is dynamic and case dependent. However, free-market rules usually apply. If you have a hot startup which everyone is dying to join and every investor throws money at you, then you have huge leverage in negotiations. On the other hand, if your startup is mediocre, you are in a weak position and have to give away much more in return for skill sets and capital. What we discuss here are just some typical situations and issues you may encounter in the process.

Smart management of the equity pool and striking a right balance is an art, and essential to the prosperity and success of the business. Also, it is something that evolves. Giving up too much equity early on ties your hands in attracting talent in the future. On the other hand, offering a tiny share of the company may hamper your ability to bring key employees on board in the early days. A simple rule of thumb is that the percentage you offer becomes smaller as the company grows and risks diminish.

Risk is the highest in the early days, and the market value of the business is minuscule or zero. That is when you need to beef up offers to potential co-founders and key employees. As time passes and the business grows and its value climbs, newcomers get a smaller slice of the pie.

Usually, the equity saga starts with the founding team when they decide to join forces and pursue an idea. Then it expands when investors, employees, and advisors come on board. Despite the nuances, a simple rule governs how much equity you trade for service or capital. And you should be okay as long as you adhere to this rule. The main rule is to exchange the expected future value of the equity in proportion to a particular contribution. The contribution is what you receive in return for giving up the equity in your business, and it must be the only determining factor in deciding how many shares to give away.

The contribution is relative, and the scope of the whole operation and team determines its value. Of course, contribution is a subjective matter and not easy to quantify. But you can ballpark by exercising due diligence and consulting with other entrepreneurs and active investors. Usually, the contribution is for a given period, typically over four years after new talent joins the startup. That is why the granted shares are vested over time, meaning an employee is entitled to a larger percentage of his shares as time passes. Usually, the employee can vest 25% of the granted shares after one year of service at the company. He or she gets more vesting as time passes. Many startups frame this in a way such that the employee receives nothing if he or she leaves the company or is let go before completing the first year.

Expected future value of the equity is how much the shares will be worth when the business reaches a particular milestone. Say your company has initially issued a million shares and you grant a new employee 10,000 shares (1% of the enterprise). Usually, the shares are worth very little in the beginning. For the sake of simplicity, let's assume each share is valued at 10 cents at the time of hire. At this valuation, the total value of his shares is $1,000 when he joins the company. However, he owns nothing in the beginning, and the grant is just a promise. Over a four-year vesting period, he will own 2,500, 5,000, 7,500, and 10,000 shares after the first, second, third, and fourth year of service. If the company does well and its valuation grows over time, then by the time the employee is fully vested (owns all his shares) the value of the shares is considerably higher. For example, the value of each share may have increased 100-fold and reached $10. In this case, the value of his shares after four years, when they are fully vested, reaches $100,000. As a successful startup usually grows quickly, the value of the employee's equity continues to increase over time and can rise 1,000-fold or more from the date of hire. That is when he joins the millionaires club. That's the whole financial promise of a startup company and a potent tool for entrepreneurs.

When we discuss ownership, what matters is the percentage of the shares and not the absolute number. The percentage is obtained by dividing the number of the shares by the total number of outstanding shares in the company. As an entrepreneur, you need to focus on the portions and different classes of the stock. I frequently encounter professionals who have no clue about this, and a larger absolute number of shares makes them happier. Once, a friend was interviewing with a handful of tech companies for a new job. He ultimately received offers from two different startup companies. He wanted to join the second company because they had offered him a larger number of shares. The first company was offering 10,000 shares, and the second was offering 100,000. He had no idea when I asked him what percentages each one translated to. Later, he realized the first offer was better because the number of outstanding shares in the first one was 1,000,000 and in the second was 20,000,000. The first company had offered him 1% equity in the enterprise compared to 0.5% of the second one.

Co-founders and Employees

It is common for co-founders to have the biggest share of the company—at least in the beginning—followed by key employees, and finally other contributors. This setup excludes investors as the deal takes a different shape with them, and we are going to discuss it shortly. The equation is easy if there is only one founder, as he or she starts out owning 100% of the equity. Entrepreneurs experience their first equity dilemma when the founding team is larger. A common practice is to divide the equity among all the founders equally. This approach is reasonable if the contributions are relatively equal.

Aside from the contribution level, there is a caveat to splitting the shares equally among the founders. It becomes especially problematic when the number of founders is even and they are all board members. For example, a two-person founding team may decide to split the shares 50-50, with both having equal voting rights as board members. This is a recipe for headaches down the road. Because any time that they don't agree on something, it creates a deadlock. On the other hand, this never happens for a team of three with equal shares (one-third each). In this situation, the best approach is to either create a 50-50 ownership but an imbalanced voting structure at the board level, where one of the board members is entitled to break a tie, or to split the shares to 51% and 49% and the voting rights are proportional to everyone's ownership.

You should be aware of unreasonable demands from potential co-founders who ask for an outsized portion of the equity. I advise you to keep the "equity proportional to relative-contribution" formula in mind and resist giving up shares just to be kind or friendly. Anyone holding a sizable chunk of equity and not pulling his weight is going to handicap the business. The same rule applies to employees as well. For example, you shouldn't split the shares 51-49, if you quit your previous job and are working full time on the startup, but your co-founder is still employed at another company and only contributes part time.

Advisors

Advisors are an enabling force in making your startup successful. A good practice is to recruit a slate of top-notch advisors who can help you with different aspects of the business. Your startup doesn't necessarily employ them as full-time employees. They usually contribute part time or on demand. You typically compensate them with equity for their contributions. The percentage of granted shares varies based on what they bring to the table. In the early stage of a startup, on average 1% to 2% for a four-year vesting period might be a good benchmark to start from, then customize based on the expected impact. The 2% is for advisors who play a key role. It is wise to hire them for one-year periods and renew after the end of their term if you are happy with their contribution. It is advisable to make sure they live up to their expected contribution or the deal is off.

Board Members

Board members appointed by investors don't take additional equity or necessarily receive any compensation from the company. The same rule applies to a founder who is also a member of the board. On the other hand, it is customary to compensate independent board members with equity. Offering a piece of the company is a compelling incentive for them to commit time and effort to advance the interests of the shareholders. As with advisors, you should make sure board members contribute and their shares vest over a period of time. How much equity to offer to a board member varies, but it is typically in the range of 0.5% to 2% over a four-year vesting period. Also, the percentage depends on the stage at which they join the board.

Investors

In each round of fundraising, investors take a chunk of equity in return for injecting capital into the enterprise. The concept is simple. Before the company starts raising capital, the founding team owns 100% of the firm. In a fundraising transaction, they sell a portion of the company to investors. Assume a company is worth $5 million. In this case, selling 30% of the startup brings in $1.5 million (= $5 million x 0.3). This transaction is the core of every fundraising round. A startup company raises capital in multiple stages, starting with a "seed" series, followed by series A, B, C and so forth. At each stage, the money is used to reach significant milestones and reduce risk. In the beginning, the risk level is the highest, and it declines with proper execution and growth of the company.

In each fundraising event, the central question is the price tag for the company. Some professionals evaluate startups and determine the total value of a company, but you must pay attention to the caveats. First, the valuation they come up with is just an estimate. Therefore, there is always room for negotiation. For example, investors may value your startup at $5 million and pay $1.5 million to take 30% of the company. But you can push back and offer only 25% for the same amount of capital, technically valuing the company at $6 million. The second caveat is the fact that it is tough to value an early stage startup because there are so many unknowns and not-yet-met, significant milestones.

As of the valuation, there are two ways to look at it. Post-money valuation refers to how much the company is worth after receiving the new funding; pre-money valuation is the value of the company before receiving the funds. The difference between post-money and pre-money valuations is the amount of funds raised.

Convertible Notes

In the early stage, the valuation is only speculative and can vary widely, which makes it difficult for the parties to agree on a particular value. In this case, entrepreneurs often raise capital through convertible notes.

A convertible note is a method commonly used to raise seed money, especially from angel investors, which we will discuss in the next chapter. The idea behind this type of transaction is to bring in money as debt which converts to equity in the future. In a sense, the investor preorders a piece of the company. As there hasn't been any valuation established at the time of the transaction and nobody knows how much the company is worth, the investor puts up money to have the right to receive the equivalent value in shares of the enterprise.

The first formal appraisal of a company, which usually happens at the time of a Series A fundraising, triggers the conversion. Until that event, the money remains as debt, and the company has an obligation to return it to the investor at a previously agreed upon rate of interest. The pre-conversion period can't go forever. There is a maturity date, at which point the company must pay back the debt with interest. If things go well, there will be a new fundraising round and, consequently, a valuation sometime down the road; that is the time when the debt converts to equity.

Seed investors take on a higher risk by investing early on, so their money has a higher value compared to new investors. These early investors get a higher value because they believed in the entrepreneurs when the company was in its infancy and merely an idea, accompanied with a passion for bringing it to life. Therefore, the investment, which was in the form of debt to the company, converts to equity at a pre-determined discount, e.g., 20%. This arrangement means the price of each share is reduced by the discount rate from the price at which the shares are assessed, or what they cost to other investors. For example, assume a startup has raised $500,000 in the form of convertible notes, and now they are doing a Series A fundraising, with each share valued at $10. With a discount rate of 20%, the cost of each share for the seed investor (debt holder) will be $8, and his $500,000 converts to 62,500 shares in the company. In comparison, $500,000 buys Series A investors only 50,000 shares.

Venture Round

The arrangement is usually different for a Series A financing. Before raising money, the equity has one form, called common stock. But the company creates preferred stocks as soon as it raises funds and brings investors on board. The preferred category gives investors priority in collecting what they own in the company ahead of holders of common stock. Technically they cash out before anyone else. When the company makes an exit, which is also called a "liquidity event"—not to be confused with a liquidation event—owners of preferred stock are first in line to receive their money. For example, when a company is acquired, preferred shareholders are paid first, and if anything is left, common stock holders take their share.

Among investors there is an order to who gets paid first. If you are familiar with basics of computer programming, you can look at this as a stack. Common shareholders are at the bottom of the stack, then come first-round investors, second-round investors, etc. Last-round investors sit on the top of the pile, and they are paid before anyone else. Then come the second-from-the-last-round investors and so on. However, there is an exception to the priority scenario, and that is when a company goes public in an IPO. In an IPO, preferred stock converts to common stock and the pool is shared among all shareholders based on their ownership in the company.

As an entrepreneur, sooner or later, you will find out that investors are diligent about protecting their interests and maximizing returns. The next chapter discusses how investors expect high returns, usually greater than ten times the money they have committed. Always, they think of all outcomes and put measures in the contract to realize their goal.

Let's look at a simple scenario of the startup we mentioned earlier. Assume the company raised $2 million in Series A from a VC firm on an $8 million post-money valuation and gave away 25% of the shares. In this case, pre-money valuation is $6 million, which is obtained by subtracting the raised capital ($2 million here) from its post-money valuation ($8 million in this example). If the startup spends all $2 million and then someone acquires it for $10 million, one may think of it as a positive outcome for the founders and perhaps for the investor as well. Only based on his ownership percentage in the company (25% here), the VC takes $2.5 million and makes $500,000 profit on the investment. But most investors don't accept such a scenario, which is very disappointing to them because the return is very low. Making $500,000 profit from a $2 million investment while the founders and the employees walk away with $7.5 million is not an acceptable outcome for professional investors.

To protect themselves from such a scenario and maximize their returns, VCs often push for a "multiple" clause, which means they get a multiple of their original investment instead of the proceeds based on their percentage of the ownership. The multiple can be any number, but two times or three times are typical. For example, in the case above, the VC secures $4 million out of the $10 million if the multiple is two (2x). After the VC takes his multiple, he either participates in the distribution of the $6 million ($10 million minus $4 million) remaining funds, or he doesn't partake. In the first case, he receives an additional $1.5 million (0.25 x $6 million) bringing his total takeaway to $5.5 million. The multiple and participating arrangement leaves only $4.5 million ($10 million minus $5.5 million) for common stock holders. If he doesn't participate, then all $6 million goes to the founders and the employees. A clause in the investment contract determines whether the VC is a "participating" or "non-participating" party. Entrepreneurs prefer a "non-participating" arrangement because it doesn't let the VC double dip and requires him to take money off the table either based on the multiple or his ownership.

In the "non-participating" case, there is a point where the proceeds based on the percentage of the ownership is equal to the one based on the multiple. In this example, the threshold is $16 million, where the 25% of the acquisition price amounts to $4 million. If the company is acquired for more than this threshold, it is more profitable for the VC to take his share of the proceeds based on ownership percentage. And if the company sells for a price below this threshold, he prefers to receive proceeds based on the multiple. To make sure they don't miss out on a blockbuster exit, investors usually put a conversion clause in the contract which grants them a right to decide whether they want to convert their preferred stock to common stock and receive proceeds based on their share of ownership. Entrepreneurs must pay close attention to the conversion rate because it is not necessarily one-to-one—and can be a higher rate, which allows the VC to take more than his original ownership percentage. For example, if the conversion rate is 1-to-2, then the number of his shares doubles.

Assume the company in the case above sells itself to an acquirer for $20 million. In a "non-participating" case, if it is just the multiple, the VC takes only $4 million for a multiple of two. Or he receives $5 million (0.25 x $20 million) if he decides to collect the proceeds only based on his 25% ownership in the company. However, in the "participating" case, he takes a total of $8 million ($4 million + 0.25 x ($20 million minus $4 million) equivalent to 40% of the proceeds. A participating clause can be very risky for entrepreneurs and can put them in a disadvantaged position by creating an enormous payoff for the investor and not much for the common stock holders. In order not to disincentivize the entrepreneurs and the employees, the contract usually includes a "cap" on the amount of money that an investor can take off the table. The cap is also a multiplier that defines the maximum takeout of an investor. For example, if the cap is three times (3x), then the investor is entitled only up to three times of his investment and no more. In our example, and for the case of $20 million acquisition and 3x cap, the VC can take only $6 million (3 x $2 million) instead of $8 million when there is no cap.

"Liquidation Preference" determines all the details of how much money an investor receives, and its priority versus other investors at the exit. Investors hold preferred shares that give them higher priority than common-stock holders to collect their promised return from the proceeds. As mentioned earlier, among preferred shareholders the first investors are usually at the end of the priority queue, and the newest investors are at the front. The last-round investors have seniority over investors in the earlier rounds because their capital helps the company to get closer to a successful exit. However, this doesn't mean the earlier investors are losers, because if the company has done well by the time it starts the new round of fundraising, the previous investors have already benefited from the increased valuation of the company. In addition to percentage of ownership, additional parameters such as the multiple, participating (versus non-participating), and the cap come into play. Please note that what we reviewed here are typical scenarios, and it is possible to have other arrangements and clauses in the contract.

As an entrepreneur, you must keep track of all liquidation preferences, and make sure you know exactly how much every entity is going to cash out in a liquidity event. The liquidation preference table gets more complicated as you raise more money and bring in more investors. I recommend you set a goal in reaching a balanced and reasonable deal with your investors. It is important to guarantee a handsome return to your investors and enough protection for their investment. At the same time, you must defend the interests of common stockholders. After presenting your business plan to a potential investor, you may receive a letter of intent expressing their interest in investing in your company. The offer has all the details we discussed here and comes in a document called a "term sheet." You should study the proposals carefully and understand the investor's liquidation preferences. Keep in mind that a term sheet is not a final offer and usually you can negotiate the terms. It is a no-brainer that having multiple offers strengthens your hand to negotiate better deals.

One thing to clarify here is the matter of voting rights, which determines control over important decisions in the company. Ownership percentage doesn't necessarily translate to the same voting or control structure.

Chapter Five

Fundraising

Up to this point, it has been all about you and your business. But when it comes to fundraising, you should put yourself in potential investors' shoes and understand what they are looking for in an investment. Many entrepreneurs are so focused and absorbed in their idea and plan that they overlook the nuances of raising funds.

Securing capital is only 20% of the job; the other 80% is to have a robust and competitive business plan. You should be in a strong position after going through the steps we covered in Chapter 2. Let's assume that your business plan fares very well on all the essential elements. However, raising money is not necessarily easy. It takes time and persistence. This chapter prepares you for meetings and contacts with potential investors. Also, you will learn about what type of investor you should go after.

In this chapter, we look at different sources that you can raise capital from, and describe how they operate. Also, we learn about the best ways to approach them and how to maximize your chances of success.

Before Approaching Investors

What investors look for

Different types of investors have different agendas. Private capital looks for a handsome return on their investment while minimizing the risks. Governments have a broader objective and usually want to fuel job creation and secure the country's leadership in technology. To succeed in a fundraising campaign, an entrepreneur needs to fully understand the investors' objectives and decide who is a good fit.

It is a selection process for both sides. You are trying to find the best investor to fund your venture and help you to achieve your objectives, and they are searching for the best investment opportunities. In this matchmaking process, you must be fully conversant on the rules and know how to play the game. Never lose your perspective on what an investor is looking for and how your business plan can be a vehicle for them to achieve their objective.

Non-Disclosure Agreement

One weekend afternoon, I got an email from my friend Sarah. I had not heard from her for quite some time. She said that things were going okay for her, and described how busy she was. Sarah had come up with a product idea and wanted to start a company. She asked me if I could review her plan and give feedback. I responded positively and said I would be happy to help. A couple of hours later she replied with a thank you message and asked me to sign an NDA before disclosing the idea. I declined to sign the NDA and told her that she was going at it in the wrong way. The only thing I did was to wish her the best of luck with her endeavor.

It is typical of inexperienced entrepreneurs contacting people for advice and feedback to ask that the advisor sign an NDA. They usually repeat that with potential investors. There are multiple reasons why this is a rookie mistake. You should avoid it and save yourself from embarrassment.

First, you shouldn't contact a person if you suspect they may steal your idea. Second, there is a good chance that the concept you are so excited about is not that original.

Third, the key to success is execution, and not necessarily the idea. It is unlikely that someone will start to build a company based on your idea, even if they find it to be brilliant. The bottom line is that you should only ask people who have official positions in your company—typically post funding—to sign an NDA.

You don't have to broadcast your idea and the business plan. Often, companies stay in "stealth mode." It is possible for people to start talking about your idea with others and the whole thing spreads around. So, when you are sharing your plan or idea with friends or people in your network, it is okay to politely ask them to be discrete and not to share with others. Or you'd better not share it at all unless necessary.

The key is to have a select group of people, preferably with experience in starting a company, and those who have in-depth knowledge of your field. If you suspect someone may compete with you or work against your interests, then you shouldn't talk to them. The same goes for potential investors. They are not going to sign an NDA, but you can be selective. Someone with a competitive business in their portfolio will most likely share your idea with that business. Great insights and feedback are priceless, and you should seek them, but be smart and selective about whom to talk to and how you approach them.

Do Your Homework

Nothing can substitute for good preparation before talking to a potential investor. Don't rush it. Make sure you have done your homework. It happens often that people get excited about their ideas and start chasing investors without sufficient preparation. That is a recipe for failure. Nobody writes you a check just by hearing about an idea.

In addition to the ten elements of a solid business plan, you must clearly and explicitly have a budget estimate and fundraising plan.

Exit Strategy

Potential investors will definitely ask you about your exit strategy. In other words, what is the endgame? Most likely this will evolve as the business grows and time passes. But you still need to have a vision about the outcome. Obviously, going public is what many entrepreneurs dream about, but it doesn't mean your business is well suited to the IPO route. You may develop technologies and a business that are very attractive to potential acquirers. Overall, you should have an idea about how things will play out in the future.

The exit strategy is important for investors because they care about getting their money back with good multiples and in a reasonable time frame.

Know Your Investor

You shouldn't look at investors simply as a source of capital. They can be extremely helpful in setting strategy at the board level, making introductions to potential customers and suppliers, facilitating the next rounds of fundraising, and recruiting key personnel. On the other hand, if you make a poor choice and bring a second-rate investor onboard, he can hamper your progress and put your success at risk. Thus, it is very important to do your due diligence before partnering with an investor.

I met Jason through a common connection a few years ago. He had founded a technology startup in California and was looking for advisors to help him with running the business. At the first meeting, I found him to be a brilliant person with a very strong technical background. After some negotiation, I accepted his invitation to join his team as an advisor. The company had a good product idea and the team was strong. They had already raised capital from a VC for a two-year runway. But the business plan wasn't perfect, and I was surprised to see how clueless their investor was about the industry and the favorable trajectory for the company. I started to help them with some shortcomings and drafting a long-term strategy. In a few months, we developed a solid product roadmap and identified possible growth opportunities. The most likely exit for the company was acquisition, so we made a list of target buyers and why Jason's company would be valuable to them.

As time went by, Jason's enthusiasm for having a supportive investor faded, and his frustration with the investor grew stronger. Despite the effort and time spent on developing the long-term plan and strategy, the VC was delaying or vetoing key decisions. The investor had a majority vote at the board and his representative didn't have any background in the company's industry. He appeared indecisive on many occasions and became a bottleneck. Jason never got any introductions to potential customers or other investors. As the next round of fundraising approached, the VC was less and less helpful. Over the course of two years, the investor changed his representative at the board of directors and the company had to spend a lot of time and energy to bring the new person up to speed. I saw firsthand how a bad match had hamstrung the company's progress.

Many first-time entrepreneurs get excited when someone shows interest in funding their venture, to the extent that they fail to do a sufficient background check. They become mostly focused on closing a round as soon as possible, and don't get to know their financial backer well. When I asked Jason about how they ended up with such a lousy VC, his answer was telling. He had stopped talking to other VCs and accepted the term sheet from the first investor who showed interest. He had not talked to the founders of the VC's other portfolio companies. It is crucial to the success of your business to establish a productive working relationship with your investors. The right course of action is to talk to the founders of some of their portfolio companies. Ask your investor for references and spend time reaching out to them. Search on the Internet and see if you can find any positive or negative publicity about them. Get informed.

Pitch Material

Elevator Pitch

A strong elevator pitch is an essential tool for all entrepreneurs, no matter what stage they are at. Simply, it's the answer you give when asked what your startup does, and it's what an aspiring company founder repeats over and over. "Elevator" is a metaphor for how long it should take you to describe the business. If you happen to share a ride on an elevator with a potential investor, you should be able to succinctly tell him or her what your business is about before they walk out. Stop here for a moment and say your spiel. Record it and then play it back a couple of times. How do you like it? Do you feel it delivers?

I have heard numerous elevator pitches, and it is not an exaggeration to say fewer than 1% were good. Most entrepreneurs understand their pitch must be short and concise, taking less than a minute to deliver. But, sadly, many elevator pitches don't have the right composition. Some of them are the result of an obsession with squeezing too much information into a 30-second timeframe and becomes a rambling speech. Others are so full of jargon that they make your head spin. A perfect pitch gets to the point and flows smoothly and naturally.

The starting point is the content. The message you want to convey is about your unique technology and solution, and who the customers are. Leave the rest of business plan out of the elevator pitch. How would you describe these aspects in a normal conversation? Write it down or record it. Do not time your pitch at this point. Do several passes, and edit it until it feels right and consistent. Then see how long the pitch is. If it is a couple of minutes and you are happy with the delivery, leave it as it is. Run it by some friends or colleagues to get feedback. Don't become obsessed with keeping it within an exact timeframe. However, you are not doing a good job if the pitch is lengthy. It is common to see entrepreneurs making their business sound more complicated than necessary. If that is the case, enlist help from others to simplify it. The bottom line is this: keep the elevator pitch simple and easy to understand.

After delivering your pitch, and depending on the situation, you may engage in a follow-up discussion or answer some questions. That is when you can tap into the content of your business summary. Or you may share your executive summary or slide deck if the person seems like a potential partner.

One-Page Executive Summary

Usually, this is the first document you share with prospective investors or potential hires. The goal is to summarize main points in a one-page document. It is a summary, not an essay. I can't stress enough the importance of keeping it to only one page and no more. More pages show a lack of proper communication skills, and it is very likely that the message will get lost. Keep in mind that your target readers don't have time or patience to read a lengthy document. The goal is to capture their attention and communicate your business plan effectively in a short period.

Another piece of advice is to avoid grandiose or superficial statements and buzz words. Otherwise, you risk your credibility and your message may ring hollow. Some power words have been overused to the extreme. How many times do you think an investor has heard words like insane, disruptive, revolutionary, and so forth, from entrepreneurs whose startups went nowhere quickly? If you have a sound, solid business plan you don't need grandiose words. I bet hearing those words from an entrepreneur-to-be makes many in the community cringe and roll their eyes. Please save yourself from the embarrassment and avoid using such words.

Appendix A shows a sample executive summary with the major sections. In the header, you should put the company name and logo – though it is not necessary for a startup to have a logo. This document is the place to introduce who you are. Also, it might be useful to identify on the right side of the header the round of funding for which you are raising money (e.g., seed round, Series A), and a date. In the main text, start by telling a bit about the company, where you are based, and what the mission is.

The next thing to address is your product and technology. You should vividly and concisely explain the problem you are solving or what service you are offering. Don't tell stories, and keep it short. Remember, readers don't know anything about your idea or business, so make sure it is clear and understandable. Explain how your product works. Don't shy away from adding a picture that shows how your product looks; nothing beats good visuals. You are not doing a good job in presenting your business if the explanation is longer than a paragraph with three or four lines.

Then, dedicate a few lines to potential customers. Who is going to buy the product? Who is itching to give you money to get your solution? This paragraph is the place to mention the results of a market study, if you have done one.

The next question that comes up is market size. This is a critical piece of information that can make or break a funding opportunity. Be truthful and make sure you have done your homework. Do not throw out random numbers or exaggerate the market opportunity. Don't foolishly try to make up astronomical figures to match big-name companies. A reasonable estimate keeps you and your team realistic and increases your chances of getting funded.

Next, explain your go-to-market strategy. Clearly, no one can serve all potential customers immediately, and clearly you need to expand your reach gradually. This approach is also called a "beachhead strategy." Show where you'll start and the plan for penetrating the market. For example, a company that develops wearable gear for athletes to improve their techniques needs to identify which sport or group is its first target. Targeting college football can be a reasonable starting point. Obviously, it's unrealistic to cover all sports or potential customers in the beginning.

Now that you have established that there is a big enough market for the product, it is time to present your business model and monetization plan. In other words, you should explain how you are going to make money.

Doing a thorough study of the competition is vital to your success, as I noted earlier. Potential investors want to know how crowded the market is. For example, the market for food bars is projected to be around $8.3 billion in 2016, with an average year-to-year growth rate of more than 6%. But there are already many competitors and a wide variety of products on the market. Or maybe there are not many competitors, but you are going against giant, entrenched companies (like competing against Johnson & Johnson if you are making a new toothpaste). The section on the competitive landscape is intended to give potential investors an idea of how much of an uphill battle it is to enter this market.

An essential element of your business plan is the unfair advantage you might have. This part is about what puts you ahead of the competition and provides a strong barrier of entry. Experienced investors always look for this in your pitch materials to assess the competitive advantage of the business.

So far it has been a run-up to what we are seeking. After making a case for your business, it's finally time to talk about how much capital you plan to raise and for how long. It still amazes me to see entrepreneurs failing to clarify the time frame. Say you are seeking $2 million. Don't you think a potential investor wants to know how long this carries your business and to what milestones? Is it for a six-month, one-year, or 18-month runway? Moreover, you need to specify what it is that you are planning to achieve by the end of this period.

The last section should be dedicated to the team. Here is the place to showcase your people. A potential investor wants to know the team, and their skill sets, to assess their potential. Co-founders and full-time employees are the key members. I have seen entrepreneurs list friends or family with big titles. My recommendation is to keep it real and only include those who are really part of the business. Having a couple of business and scientific advisors is a good idea too.

Finally, I like to put contact info in the footer. And don't forget to proofread the document and ask for feedback before distributing it to potential investors.

Summary Slide Deck

Some entrepreneurs prefer a summary deck to a one-pager. A slide deck is a collection of slides made with a presentation program such as Microsoft PowerPoint or Apple Keynote. It serves the same purpose as a one-pager. Again, you send it to potential investors—preferably in pdf format—or share it with major partners to pique their interest. The purpose is to secure a follow-up meeting for further discussion and to present the main slide deck. At this stage, the audience usually reads the slides on their own, or you present them at a pitch event where you have about two minutes to introduce your business to a panel of investors. So, it is essential to make sure they are self-explanatory. Your target audience should be able to go through them quickly and get the key points. I personally prefer a slide deck to an executive summary. You have more space and can add visuals. Having excellent figures, charts, and pictures is priceless. The deck should not be lengthy or verbose, it must be clear and easily understandable. A good number is five to eight slides. Like the executive summary, the deck must include essential information about your business plan.

Having a well-prepared deck always pays off. However, you should resist the temptation to cram a lot of material into every single slide. You should avoid anything that makes it harder to understand or overwhelms the viewer. Alex is founder of a healthcare startup which I have been advising since 2016. He is an accomplished and highly respected scientist in his field. I was shocked when I received his slide deck for review. It was so crowded that there was no way to understand and follow the story. In some of the slides he had used so many colors that it gave me a headache just to look at them. Also, he had used a gray background for which made the slides look depressing. He put a logo of his company at the upper right corner of each slide—I don't believe you need to have a logo at all—and in a couple of his slides, the logo also appeared in the content, creating an unpleasant visual. We ended up spending hours fixing the slide deck and making it into something presentable.

The rule of thumb for making good slides is to have just one key point in each slide and no more. Don't overuse colors and don't overcrowd with content. Keep them neat, readable, and easy on the eyes. Cramming a lot of material into each slide doesn't make them better or more professional, it makes you look like someone who doesn't know how to present. Potential investors evaluate you not only for the viability of the business, but also for your presentation skills. It is expected of an entrepreneur to interact with different parties and make a case for the business. Not being able to make a good impression in that regard reduces your chances of getting funded. Meetings with investors, customers, and potential employees are not only about the business or product, but also about the founder who runs the company.

Visuals and drawings are compelling tools that many entrepreneurs ignore or pay little attention to. These days, most interactions happen in short time spans, and nothing captures an audience's attention and relays the message like great drawings and pictures. Often, a page full of text can be replaced with one figure that conveys all the information. You don't need to have precise and professional drawings. Even a good drawing made by hand can be sufficient.

Main Slide Deck

Investors will invite you for an in-person meeting if they become interested in your business plan. This session happens after they go through your summary (one-pager or summary deck) and find it attractive. The invitation is a great opportunity, and you should make the best out of it. Make sure you are thoroughly prepared and have answers to possible questions. You may not receive funding at the meeting, but it is a significant step towards securing capital. For this session, you need a detailed slide deck where you elaborate on various aspects of the business plan. Have a few copies of the main deck and take them to the meeting, because there might not be a projector, computer, or notebook screen to present the slides, or you may only have a conversation.

In addition to elaborating on the aspects mentioned in the summary deck, you should discuss your budget, timeline, and milestones. Market research and customer surveys are golden. Methodically outline all key aspects of the business plan. Be prepared to address the questions they might have. This encounter is your opportunity to walk out of the meeting triumphantly, so don't flounder. A good practice is to do dry runs with friends and colleagues before an investor meeting.

A good place to get some ideas about a professional main slide deck is LinkedIn's Series B pitch. The slide deck is public, and you can easily find it by searching for the title. I suggest downloading and carefully going through the slides. It is not for the first round of fundraising and the content is a bit different, but you can obtain great insights to a proper structure and format.

Sources of Capital

A mistake many entrepreneurs make is that they are solely focused on what they want from investors. They think investors will share their excitement and write them a check as soon as they hear about the idea. That's not how they operate. You'd better change your mindset and understand what potential investors are typically looking for, what their goals are, and how your company can help them succeed in their business. When you are looking for someone to invest in your business, you should learn about whom to talk to and whether your venture is attractive to them.

You may have a short time in mind to reach an early milestone, build a quick prototype, or test the market and gain some users. If you are looking for funding to do a proof of concept in a few months, then your best options are: self-funding, raising money from friends and family, or making a deal with angel investors. Focusing on these options saves you a lot of time that you'd otherwise have to spend on fundraising. For larger sums—Series A and onward—you should approach VCs, although you may find some VCs who invest in seed rounds as well.

Bootstrapping

Most entrepreneurs end up doing some form of bootstrapping or self-funding. One reason is the difficulty of raising money with only a plan on paper or PowerPoint slides. Having proof of concept before diving into a full-fledged operation and getting involved in the fundraising process can be advantageous. This approach usually increases the chances of raising capital or speeds it up. Also, if executed well, potential investors will be more receptive to your pitch.

The main risk of self-funding is depleting your savings or racking up a large debt. You can quickly ruin your finances and become desperate to raise capital. Having poor personal finances increases your stress level and consequently reduces your productivity. Do not be careless or adventurous with your money. Often it is not a good idea to go into debt to fund your startup. Remember, more than 90% of startups fail. The prospect of being broke and having a failed venture at hand is not attractive.

You have probably heard stories or watched movies about highly successful people who mortgaged their homes, or racked up large balances on their credit cards, or depleted their retirement and savings accounts, to pursue their dream and ultimately make it big. Those are exceptions and perhaps more dramatized than what they were in reality. I don't recommend you take such a massive risk and end up being broke.

You may have already quit your job. Forgoing a steady income along with spending all your time and effort is a substantial risk that you have already taken. Besides, often you must forgo other opportunities that come your way (opportunity cost). If you conclude that it is in your interest to self-fund the operation for a limited time, then set a definite limit and be disciplined about not crossing that threshold. For example, if you have $20,000 in savings, then never spend more than $10,000 bootstrapping your business. If you need more money, the best course of action is to raise capital. There is plenty of capital in the market chasing promising business plans. If your plan checks against all the fundamental elements, then you should be able to raise money to fund the startup.

Friends & Family

Raising money from a friend or relative is still a form of partnership, but a different kind. I cautioned against recruiting people with close personal ties. The same advice goes for raising money. It is great that your loved ones have respect and admiration for you, or you have friends who trust you and are willing to invest in your company. But think twice about it and resist the temptation. You are putting your relationship at risk and may regret it in the future.

People are willing to invest in your business in anticipation of a big return. It is likely that they are tapping their own hard-earned savings or retirement money. They are usually not savvy investors, and their investment in your business is more emotional than logical. This situation adds an extra dimension and a significant emotional factor to the arrangement. It is not only a business transaction but an emotional one too. If you are successful and return their investment with impressive multiples, then everybody is happy, and they will love you even more. On the other hand, most likely your relationship will take a blow and suffer if the opposite happens. Again, more than 90% of startups fail. Not that that is going to be the fate of your startup, but the odds are not in your favor.

It takes time to build a business, and friends and family might not be sufficiently patient due to a lack of understanding of the process. Usually, their sense of the process is based on rare success stories and how the founders and financial backers became wealthy overnight. Just be mindful and assess how you would deal with the situation if the business turns out to be a flop. On the flip side, raising money from people you know can be easier and faster than turning to professional investors. Quick access to capital can propel your startup to the prototype or proof-of-concept stage in a short time. Also, being responsible to loved ones can enhance your motivation and diligence.

Crowdfunding

With crowdfunding, a relatively new avenue for raising capital, the money comes from many participating investors, usually through an Internet platform. Most of them are ordinary people who invest small amounts of money, usually less than a hundred dollars. Entrepreneurs typically raise amounts ranging from thousands to hundreds of thousands of dollars on those platforms. The transaction is often done through a broker who charges a fee, something around 5%. If you raise $10,000, they take a $500 cut, and you will end up with $9500 in your bank account. Crowdfunding investors usually don't get any equity in the company. Instead, they receive the product earlier than anybody else. Such people are early adopters or people who like to support an idea.

There are several crowdfunding platforms, including Kickstarter, IndieGoGo, and GoFundMe. The allure of crowdfunding is not giving away equity and not having investors breathing down your neck and meddling in your business. However, you are committing yourself to production and sending the product to contributors.

Nowadays, there are tons of projects running crowdfunding campaigns. To be successful, you need to run a competitive marketing campaign and be able to do a successful promotion. Not long ago, I was driving back to San Francisco after a meeting in Silicon Valley when, to my surprise, I saw an advertisement for a crowdfunding project on a billboard on U.S. Highway 101 close to San Francisco International Airport. Obviously running a crowdfunding campaign takes money and time. Therefore, before jumping on one of these sites, you'd better do an excellent analysis of whether crowdfunding is a suitable vehicle to fund your business.

Generally, crowdfunding can be a great source of capital for projects with limited market size and customer base. I met Stephane for the first time in Paris at a friend's party. He is a talented photographer and had started working on an interesting project. He was creating an abstract atlas of the world with pictures he had taken of a variety of subjects in different parts of the world. He funded his project through Kickstarter and ran a successful campaign. Stephane raised €17,783 from 144 backers, exceeding his original goal of €13,000. Pledging €10 would have gotten you an image from the book. I received a signed copy of the full book by contributing €60.

Incubators

Incubators are for-profit companies that provide support for early-stage startups, helping them get their business off the ground. Support usually includes office space, mentorship, seed money, assistance with fundraising, making introductions to potential customers, and so forth. In return, incubators often take a stake in the company. There are many incubators, and some of them are very competitive with low admission rates.

Joining an incubator can be invaluable for first-time entrepreneurs as they get the opportunity to learn from people with years of experience. It is like an all-inclusive package vacation that helps you move forward quickly. You can interact with other entrepreneurs and learn from each other. Many times, a fellow engineer or entrepreneur can give you a tip about solving a problem with your code or design that you would normally spend quite some time on without any progress. Also, some incubators are physically located at the center of the action, such as Silicon Valley.

Physical proximity to many tech companies, other startups, entrepreneurs, VCs, and world-class engineers and experts can be invaluable.

Several incubators are managed and funded by major technology companies. These established firms have selfish motives for being in the incubator business. One way in which established companies maintain their growth, technology portfolios and competitive advantage is through mergers and acquisitions (M&A). Sometimes big players will compete to acquire a smaller company. One incentive for running an incubator is to have priority in acquiring the startups they back, or prevent them from being acquired by their competitors. Often, they put clauses in their term sheets that give them priority to acquire the startup or block anyone else from buying it. Thus, this avenue can be a double-edged sword. Your incentives and theirs may not align in forgoing a potential acquisition by one of their competitors. On the other hand, you have prime access to their business units and key decision makers, and that could boost your chances of selling your startup company to them.

Angel Investors

Some successful entrepreneurs who have already made their fortunes become "angel investors." They have valuable business experience, especially in founding a startup and making a successful exit. Investing in early stage startups is something they pursue as a full-time or part-time activity. They are an excellent source of capital for early stage startups. Angel investors typically invest tens to hundreds of thousands of dollars. They are the first group of professional investors that you may pursue. By definition, angels commit smaller amounts of capital compared to venture capitalists, and they usually invest their own money. Sometimes they partner with other angel investors to fund a startup company.

Angels are professional investors, and they must be accredited. In the U.S., accredited investors must meet certain requirements, such as minimum net worth and income. The rules are defined by the Securities and Exchange Commission (SEC), and sometimes by state agencies. There are good reasons to raise capital from angel investors. First, there are many of them, and you have a large pool of people to tap for investment in your business. Second, they are professionals who know the ins and outs of the trade. Third, unlike friends or family, you are bound by a contract, and the relationship is transactional. Fourth, they are usually seasoned entrepreneurs who can help you with your business and also make introductions to potential customers or future investors, such as VCs. If you decide to raise money from angel investors, it is prudent to make sure they are legitimate and have complied with securities laws. Also, you should consult an attorney before signing a deal.

Venture Capital

I met Mary at an entrepreneurship event in San Francisco in late 2013. She was very enthusiastic about her business idea and asked for my advice on which VCs to pursue and how to approach them. Her idea was to launch a new line of women's clothing with unique designs and made of organic cotton. The interesting part was the fact that she was planning to raise VC money. Her market analysis showed the business would reach its peak revenue of a few million dollars in three years. My first question was why she thought it was a VC-fundable business. Mary said she planned to raise $350,000 for a two-year runway to positive revenue. She was under the impression that putting in this money and then having a business with just a few million dollars annual revenue would lure many VCs. It took me almost an hour to explain why she shouldn't pursue VC funding.

Venture capital firms are the prime source of funding for U.S. startup companies. In 2016, they invested $69.1 billion in 7,751 companies. Some first-time entrepreneurs infer from this massive scale that VCs are the preferred source of capital for anyone who wants to start a for-profit business. That's not true. Competent VCs are extremely focused and disciplined about the companies they choose. You will be successful and very efficient in your fundraising if you know how they operate. Entrepreneurs usually set themselves up for failure or struggle because they don't have a good grasp of VC mechanics.

VCs operate by the principle of investing in high-risk, high-reward startup companies. Managing partners run these firms, and they decide how to deploy the money. Unlike angel investors, they do not spend their own money. Their funds come from other investors, called limited partners (LPs). A VC firm creates a fund, which could range from a few million to a few hundred million dollars, and LPs put their money in. Venture capital LPs are typically large institutional investors like pension funds, university endowments, and sovereign wealth funds. In short, LPs invest in VC funds, and the VCs in turn invest in startup companies. As money moves through this chain, it is divided into smaller chunks and deployed to a larger number of entities (the startups).

The story begins with big institutional investors. Their fiduciary responsibility is to put the money under their management to work and make it grow. That means making smart investments to secure good returns. With many billions of dollars under management (Norway's government pension fund, for example, manages over $1 trillion in assets), these entities don't bother with small investments. They deploy hundreds of millions or billions of dollars across a range of asset classes and a range of risk, including venture capital funds. One opportunity institutional money managers find attractive is to invest as LPs in multiple VC firms with the prospect of significant returns.

In 2016, Andreessen-Horowitz, a well-known Silicon Valley VC, raised $1.5 billion from LPs for their fifth fund (Fund V). Usually, a VC fund is capitalized by more than one LP. Some VC firms have outstanding reputations, generally based on their home runs (Andreesen-Horowitz invested in Facebook and Twitter before they went public, for example) and they bring in big chunks of money faster than others. After receiving the money, a VC invests in several startup companies. The mandate of a VC firm is to grow their capital and deliver outsized returns to their own partners and their LPs. In the process, VC firms charge a fee, commonly 2% of assets under management per annum; they also get a cut of the profits, which is typically 20%. VCs make their profit by investing in startup companies, obviously in those with promising futures, when those companies exit by going public or being acquired.

There are many books about what kind of startup companies VCs invest in or how to approach a VC, and so on. But VCs have a straightforward goal. Assume a VC invests A dollars in a startup company and the company returns ($N x A) over T period. Here, N is the multiplier on the original investment and T is how long it takes for the startup to exit (acquisition or IPO). VCs look for large N and short T, meaning a significant return over a short time. It is very similar to investing your savings by purchasing equities in the stock market. Clearly, you'd love to see the stock price soar over a short time. Everybody dreams of a large and speedy return on their investment.

So, clearly a VC firm only invests in a startup company if they see potential for a significant return in a short time. That's where the fundamental elements of your business plan come into play. A potential investor evaluates your proposal and decides if it fits these requirements. You may ask what an attractive multiplier is. The short answer is larger than ten times (10x)—but some people set the bar much higher, at 30x. From an individual investor's perspective, a much smaller return, say two times, seems spectacular. So why 10x? Remember, VCs have to return capital to their LPs with big profits. They also take an annual management fee from the fund, so the net amount of money available for investment is less than what they have raised from LPs. Moreover, despite thorough evaluations and analyses, still many of a VC's portfolio startups fail, and they usually have to write off those investments. Ultimately it falls on the shoulders of a few successful ones to make up for the flops, cover the management fees and deliver a profit. This way the return on the fund becomes positive, the VC can take a cut of the profits, and it also makes good on its promise of delivering a significant return to the LPs. That's why a business plan that falls short of making a compelling case for a strong performance has little or no chance of receiving VC funding.

If your business plan doesn't support more than a 10x return over a reasonable period, you might be better off pursuing other forms of funding instead of trying to raise capital from VCs. Some entrepreneurs lose perspective and think their great idea automatically merits investment from VCs. They spend a lot of time and effort chasing them with no success. That's why a large market and potential for outsized growth are crucial if you want to seek this type of investors. They like scalable businesses that can ultimately deliver eye-popping returns. They hunt for startups with possible "hockey stick" (exponential) growth. If your company doesn't need a lot of capital or the potential growth is modest and not exponential, you'd better look elsewhere for money, like a loan from the Small Business Administration (SBA) or raising capital from angel investors.

VC funds have a lifespan of 10 years. It is not unusual for a VC to manage multiple funds with different maturity dates in parallel. Typically, when a fund is in its early years the managing partners take higher risks and invest more in early stage startups. As a fund gets closer to its maturation date, VCs generally use the remaining money to deploy more financial resources to their existing portfolio of companies or invest in firms that are already experiencing exponential growth. As a rule of thumb, it is good for early-stage startups to raise money from a relatively new fund.

If your business passes the test of being a VC-fundable venture, your next job is to make a list of which ones to contact. Don't reach out to everyone you have heard of or read about. It is imperative to look for those who are active in your field and have stellar reputations. Some entrepreneurs chase big- name VCs without knowing whether they play in their target industry. If not, don't waste your time and energy. Before contacting someone at a VC firm, research their portfolio and target industries. Learn about the firm and the person with whom you are planning to speak. Understand if your business is a good match to what they look for. If a VC is heavily invested in software and you are a hardware company, then it is going to be a waste of time to pursue them.

Identify your sector and find reputable firms who are actively investing in that area.

After narrowing down your list of potential investors, it is time to talk about how to contact your target VCs. First, and before contacting them, you must do your homework and have pitch material ready. Things can move very fast, and you may lose a great opportunity if not prepared. I have seen new entrepreneurs who, out of the blue, e-mailed their one-pager or summary deck to their target VCs. First, don't email any pitch material before they ask for it. Second, save cold calling as the last option. Be smart about how you pursue a target investor.

It is always preferable to find a common connection with your target VC and ask for a referral. See if any friends, family, former colleagues, fellow entrepreneurs, neighbors, classmates, or university professors, know a partner at the firm. It is better if these people know you well and are willing to make a genuine recommendation. This approach is probably the best way to reach out to your target. Then, send your pitch material if the partner asks for the summary. If he finds it attractive, he will invite you to an in-person meeting where you can present or discuss your business plan in detail. Hopefully, everything goes well, and you will receive a letter of intent. The letter means they want to invest in your business. If you don't hear back, it means they're not interested and you should move on.

It is common to fail to find any connections with your target investor and have no one to make an introduction. In this case, search for events where you may have a chance to meet them. VCs attend or present at many entrepreneurship events and conferences. Don't forget alumni events. These are also excellent opportunities to speak with target investors. I have met and chatted with a good number of prominent investors at such events. Typically, they ask about your business, and you give the elevator pitch. If they are interested, they will give you their contact information and ask for a summary or more. I don't recommend following up with them if your pitch didn't pique their interest.

It doesn't hurt to directly e-mail your target VC if you have exhausted other avenues. Just keep the message short and to the point. One or two lines of explanation about your business are sufficient. Raising money is a game that requires persistence and patience. It takes time and effort to close a deal.

Corporate Ventures

Many large enterprises have venture arms that invest in startup companies. These include Intel Capital, Microsoft Ventures, and GV (formerly Google Ventures), to name a few. Usually, the primary goal of a corporate investment division is to gain priority in acquiring complementary technologies and stay on top of the technology trends and innovations. Also, they generate some profit for the parent company. Corporate ventures can be an option for raising money, and you should consider them. They generally operate like VCs but occasionally invest in breakthrough technologies, even if those don't have a clear path for exponential growth. You should talk to them if you think their parent company can be a customer or your technology can be a strategic addition to their portfolio. Also, they usually invest in solutions that advance their product or technology ecosystems. For example, Samsung Next may invest in startups that develop apps for their smartwatches. If your product is part of an ecosystem pushed by a tech giant, then you should consider raising capital from their investment arm.

In addition to providing capital, corporate ventures offer access to the company's management and business units. Their insights and help can be instrumental in developing your technology. And you have a higher chance of being acquired by the company. On the other hand, taking money from a corporate venture may restrict your future options because they sometimes ask for priority in acquiring the company or the right to block an acquisition by a competitor. These restrictions often deter VCs from investing in the startup because the parent company might not necessarily be focused on maximizing financial returns to shareholders. It is typical for VCs to ask a corporate venture to remove such restrictive clauses before they invest in a startup.

Keep in mind that many corporate investment arms invest in a wide range of technologies, and they are not only focused on what their parent company makes. Consider corporate investments as one avenue for raising capital, but don't limit yourself to them. In general, raising money from a VC is a less restrictive option, and you can be confident that their only agenda is maximizing financial returns.

Government Grants

Many national and local governments have programs to support entrepreneurs in the form of tax incentives, training or mentorship, incubation programs, funding, and so forth. They can be a valuable resource to help get your business off the ground. The primary goal of these programs is to foster entrepreneurship. Rather than direct profits from backing startup companies, governments look for long-term payoffs in the form of economic growth, employment, and technology leadership. Government programs may not ask for any equity in return for their support, but the process can be lengthy, slow, and bureaucratic, and involves extra overhead and paperwork.

SBIR/STTR

Two main programs in the U.S. are Small Business Innovation Research (SBIR) and Small Business Technology Transfer (STTR). Twelve Federal agencies participate in the program, and they invest millions of dollars in promoting innovation in the country. The participating organizations are the Small Business Administration (SBA), the Department of Agriculture (USDA), the Department of Commerce (DoC), the Department of Defense (DoD), the Department of Education, the Department of Energy (DoE), the National Institutes of Health (NIH), the Department of Homeland Security (DHS), the Department of Transportation (DoT), the Environmental Protection Agency (EPA), the National Aeronautics and Space Administration (NASA), and the National Science Foundation (NSF). Each agency only covers fields related to their mission.

SBIR and STTR programs typically have three phases. In summary, Phase-I is a feasibility study and preliminary research.

Phase I grants are usually capped to $125,000 or $225,000 for six-month to one-year periods, depending on the agency and its objectives. The company can apply for Phase-II after completing the Phase-I and meeting the requirements for a Phase-II proposal. A typical Phase-II grant is $750,000 for two years. This phase is the period for building a commercial product and securing customers. Only a few programs accept and fund Phase-III proposals. Phase-III is for mass production and expanding market share, and it is expected of the company to have private investors. The idea is that the awardees have eliminated significant risks to their business and they are in shape to attract private capital.

SBIR is the key program for startup companies, and it is what you should consider first. You may apply for STTR if you work in partnership with a university or a research institute. In such cases, the IP comes out of the university or institute, or you find it beneficial to form a collaboration with those institutes.

The positive side of partnering with a university is access to research facilities that usually are equipped with expensive, state-of-the-art equipment. You might be able to hire postdocs or grad students to help with research and development. Despite these benefits, some disadvantages may deter you from entering such a partnership. First, the university will have a claim to the intellectual property, and you ultimately would have to license it from them.

Second, many charge a hefty administrative fee that leaves a small amount of the funds for the team that is doing the research. Third, you must manage and deal with extra overhead and paperwork. Fourth, you don't have full control over how the academic team works and acts.

I suggest against applying for STTR if your idea and IP hasn't come out of work and research at a university in the first place. Forming such a partnership without an established history is a significant risk and can seriously slow you down and hamper your progress. Possible benefits do not outweigh the risks and extra overhead.

To start the process, you should look at solicitations from sponsoring agencies. Each agency has its own SBIR website, and you should keep in mind that the formats and timelines are not the same across agencies. For example, the format and proposal submission processes are different for NASA, DoD, NSF, et. al. After identifying your target agency, carefully track and read solicitations. You can check them either on their websites or search on www.sbir.gov. I strongly recommend starting early and leaving plenty of time for preparing and submitting your proposal. As someone with a history of completing many tasks at the last minute, I assure you this is not one of them. This simply cannot be done in a short period of time because they require a lot of documentation and supporting material.

The agencies accept proposals within certain time windows, and they are very strict about deadlines and windows. Proposals must follow well-defined formats and include specifically required documents. Submitting an executive summary or a slide deck does not work in this case. Preparing a competitive proposal takes considerable time and energy—that is one reason why I prefer private investors. In addition to a detailed plan, you need to submit supporting documents, such as a very detailed expense analysis and how you are planning to spend the money. In a nutshell, there are numerous rules and requirements that you should read about and become familiar with before submitting anything. Those are lengthy documents that sometimes can be intimidating. Consulting with people who have experience can be quite useful.

Upon becoming an awardee, your business becomes a Federal government contractor. Therefore, you need to do some preparation before being able to submit a proposal. First, you must get a D-U-N-S number for your business from Dun & Bradstreet. Obtaining the number is free, and it usually takes a few business days. Next, you need to register your business with Small Business Administration and get your ID number. Then you must register at

System for Award Management (SAM). It is wise to complete these registrations at least one month before the submission deadline.

An agency will start the review process after the submission deadline. They assemble a panel of experts in the field (typically four people for a particular proposal) and ask them to examine the proposal's merits regarding originality, innovation, team, facilities, market size and commercial opportunity. It typically takes six months for the panel to complete its reviews and announce award winners. And this doesn't include the proposal preparation and submission period. This long review process is another important factor to take into consideration before committing yourself and your team to submitting a proposal. You must decide if the timeline makes sense for your business or not. On top of that, the acceptance rate is not very high, your chances will be 10% to 15%.

Overall, the complicated process to prepare a proposal, the long processing time, and low acceptance rate are disadvantages. On the other hand, the money comes with few strings attached and no equity dilution.

Small Business Administration Loans

Sometimes you need a loan to get your business off the ground and generate revenue. Probably the most famous success story of turning a small business loan into a billion-dollar company is Chobani. The founder, Hamdi Ulukaya, saw an ad for a recently closed yogurt plant in New York. He bought the plant and started his business with a loan from the SBA. The best resource to learn about SBA services is their website, www.sba.org where you can find a wealth of information. SBA is an independent agency of the Federal government, and its task is to assist and protect the interests of small businesses. Their stated mission is helping Americans start, build, and grow businesses. One of the services they offer is securing competitive loans for small businesses.

Taking a loan can be a good option for business ideas which will generate cash quickly. These are usually companies that can stay private for a long time and have a healthy and profitable business. For tech startups, a loan is not typically a good source of funding in the early days. Banks give loans to companies that have the means to make their monthly payments, and that only happens when a company has revenue.

Chapter Six

Operations

Starting a business is not simply about building a product. Paperwork and administrative tasks begin with the inception of a new company. An entrepreneur must deal with such issues as licenses, accounting, taxes, human resources, and so forth. Most entrepreneurs learn about them through trial and error, which can be costly and time consuming. In this chapter, we briefly review some of the important aspects of starting a company to help you be efficient.

Initial Expenses

Even if you start a firm in your garage, still there is some cost associated with founding a business. Foremost are the legal and registration fees for incorporating a business. Having an online presence, getting licenses from local authorities, printing business cards, acquiring necessary devices and equipment like laptops or printers, and building a prototype, are just a few of the initial expenses. On top of that, you most likely will have to pay city or state franchise taxes whether or not you're generating revenue or are profitable. I advise making a spreadsheet and listing expenses and the deadlines to ensure you are not missing anything and don't have to pay penalties in the future.

Registrations & Licenses

Many states, counties, and cities require a business to obtain a permit or license, and it needs to be renewed annually. Make sure you are familiar with the requirements and address them in a timely fashion. For example, if you operate in San Francisco, the city requires you to obtain a Business Registration Certificate and renew it every year. Depending on your line of business, you may need to get a license as well. Also, you must file a Statement of Information with the Secretary of State every year. There is a fee associated with each filing, and it varies depending on your state and city. A good practice is to add all the registrations and renewals with their corresponding deadlines as a tab to the spreadsheet you make for the expenses. This way you won't lose track of them and won't incur penalties.

Tracking progress

You can quickly lose track of progress and priorities when you are your own boss. Remember, you are managing a business, and it is your job to regularly check the status and write down action items for everyone on the team. The best practice is to schedule and hold a regular weekly meeting with the team to review things and list progress, issues, and action items. When you list action items, it is better to set a deadline and specify who is assigned to the task. One way to do it is with a simple note shared via email with everyone, or on a shared Microsoft Excel file, or an online service like Asana. Also, you can use project management software like Microsoft Project or other online services, but make sure that adds value to your operation, and it is not excessive. The key is to pick something that works best for your team.

I used to work in an R&D group designing wireless integrated circuits. Our manager was obsessed with tracking progress, and we had status meetings every morning. The team sat together in a conference room, and he would project Excel sheets on the wall. He would go through each item and check with every team member about how much progress they had made, and the details of their work. Every meeting was at least one hour. R&D is a slow process, and things don't change much in a day. Also, more than ten people had to sit, tired and bored, while he went through the details of each team member's status. We all were stuck there and could have done something useful while he was playing with his spreadsheet and moving rows and columns around or changing cells. It was a big waste of time for all of us just at the expense of his obsession. I quit the group because I felt we were wasting time for no reason.

Make sure your status meetings are well planned and not too frequent or on an irregular schedule. You are holding back a group of people from doing their jobs, so it is important to be mindful and run effective and efficient meetings. I believe an important measure of productivity is the effectiveness of meetings. Make sure you have a clear agenda for every meeting, share it with the team members in advance, and stick to it during the meeting.

Record Keeping

One thing that can get out of hand very quickly is record keeping. As an entrepreneur and businessman, it is necessary to adhere to a strict routine to keep records for all transactions and legal documents. One-time items like articles of incorporation, bylaws, employee contracts and NDAs, tax numbers, etc. must be kept in a safe place. There are recurring documents, like minutes of board meetings, tax returns, and expense receipts that you have to keep as well. Very quickly, you will find yourself buried in a mountain of paper that takes up ample storage space. Also, some of the documents, such as receipts, are thermal printouts that fade over time. I strongly recommend implementing an electronic record-keeping system. A valuable investment for your business is a multi-purpose printer. Not only can you print and copy with it, but you can also scan paper documents. After trying different options, I came to appreciate the value of a small office multipurpose laser printer.

Converting paper documents to electronic files makes it much easier to preserve and find them. In addition to having local copies and backup, uploading most of the records to a reliable cloud-based storage brings peace of mind and makes your life easier. Cloud storage creates redundancies and keeps copies of your folders in different locations. For example, if there is a natural disaster at one location, your files are still safe and accessible. As an entrepreneur, it is a good habit to scan every document or receipt and have a well-organized method for keeping them.

It may not sound like a top priority compared to building a product, but you would be surprised how ignoring small but essential things like this can make your life miserable. It is smart to use and take advantage of the latest technologies to improve productivity and efficiency.

Finance & Accounting

Unless you are disciplined and knowledgeable on how to manage your finances, I strongly recommend hiring a professional accountant. It pays off in the long run. In the beginning, you can hire a part-time accountant and avoid incurring a significant expense. It doesn't cost you much because he or she is probably going to spend only a few hours on your business per month. It's a huge help to have someone taking care of bookkeeping and organizing your finances. Usually, they can assist you with tax returns as well. For my business, I did the accounting and tax returns myself. I spent a lot of time learning about the nuances and what is acceptable as a business expense. In the end, I wasn't confident that I did things properly and ended up hiring a professional accountant. His work was more accurate and better than mine. It was then I realized that my time would be better spent running the business, developing the product, and managing team members rather than doing every little thing myself. It is okay to do some of this stuff yourself for a short time if you are running on a lean budget. But you can raise capital and pay for these expenses if you have a solid business plan.

Taxes

The step regarding taxes is to obtain an EIN (Employer Identification Number) from the IRS. You can do it online, and the process is quite straightforward. For all matters related to corporate and personal taxes, I strongly advise you to speak with a professional. Our goal in this section is to remind you of your obligations. You may need to pay federal, state, and city taxes based on your place of incorporation and where you operate. For example, if you are incorporated in Delaware and are headquartered in California, you must pay taxes to both states. Therefore, it is necessary to have a good tax plan in place and be diligent about your obligations. For starters, take a look at "Small Business Taxes: The Virtual Workshop" offered on the Internal Revenue Service's (IRS) website at https://www.irsvideos.gov/Business/virtualworkshop. The lessons are neatly organized to help you understand the basics of Federal tax law for small businesses and startups. As mentioned, you must consult with your local and state tax authorities or a Certified Public Accountant (CPA) to fully understand the rules and obligations.

Bank Accounts & Credit Cards

After incorporating your business and having all the registration documents and getting your EIN, you can open a checking or savings account with the bank of your choice. I strongly recommend separating your personal and business finances. It's good to shop around and see which banks offer the best services and deals. These days many banks offer a broad range of services for business clients, such as checking, savings, 401k, and payroll. If you don't need all of them immediately, it is still a good idea to have options for the time when your business grows. Make a comparison table and compare fees and their services before making a final decision. Some banks even offer bonuses or other incentives if you open accounts with them. Always ask about promotions.

Also, it is an excellent practice to use a business credit card specifically for business expenses. There are many business credit cards, and most of them offer reward programs. The best practice is to compare their fees, rates, and rewards to see which one works for you. If you travel a lot, then you may find it useful to get a card that offers extra rewards for travelers and perhaps access to airport lounges.

Online Presence

Website

Having an online presence enhances the image of your business and makes it look professional. It's also an excellent way to promote your products and recruit talent. A good website can work as a window into the business. However, it's better not to invest too much in an online presence if it doesn't have a direct and visible impact on the product or customer acquisition. For example, a website is an essential part of a service like Airbnb, but not so critical for a startup building a product for self-driving cars. These days, it is universal for a startup to have a website, unless for good reasons you are planning to stay in stealth mode.

To build a website, first, you need to obtain a domain name which, preferably, is precisely your business name. However, it is tough to get a good domain name without paying a lot of money. Search for different variations on one of the domain name and hosting companies like godaddy.com or domains.google. If the name is not too generic and familiar, the cost of buying the domain is relatively small, in the order of $10 to $20 per year. For example, when I wanted to register a domain name for myself (BabakSoltanian.com), I searched a provider's website and saw it was available. Then I purchased the rights to the domain for a specific length of time.

The next step is to get a hosting service to host your website. Having the domain name doesn't mean you have a website, and you must purchase hosting services as well. Buying these services from a single provider makes your life easier and saves you time. A hosting service provides storage and space for your website, and it directs every inquiry made to your domain name to the stored content. In my case, I use a hosting service to hold my website, which responds anytime someone types BabakSoltanian.com into their web browser.

After registering the domain name and purchasing a hosting service, you need to create content for your website. That is where website design comes into play. You can either hire someone to do it for you or put it together yourself. In the latter case, you need to learn some basics. Many online courses or books can teach you the basics. You don't need to know or become fluent in web programming languages like

HTML, CSS, JavaScript, etc. Use readymade templates like WordPress to quickly create something, and that should be sufficient in most cases.

Email

After securing your desired domain name, you can set up e-mail accounts. To do so, you need to buy e-mail service from a provider. Many web hosting companies offer additional services like e-mail, calendar, cloud storage, etc. Establishing an email account is not expensive, and I highly recommend it if you want to look professional.

Social Media

Social media presence can be an effective way to promote your service or product and stay in touch with customers. First, you must determine why your business needs to have an active presence on social media. It is not necessary for every business, at least in the beginning. It makes sense if you are in a consumer market and want to sell to individuals. But if you are in business-to-business (B2B) market, most likely there is no immediate need for a presence in social media. You may want to reserve the names that you think will come in handy in the future but don't spend much time on this unless there is a real business need for it.

How to adequately present your business on social media, or do search engine optimization (SEO), is a whole different topic that is beyond the scope of this book. There are excellent books and online courses regarding this subject that you can study on your own. Also, you may hire professionals who do this for a living and know all the particulars.

Human Resources

Hiring

An entrepreneur typically works with people within different frameworks, and human resources is one of the things that he or she will deal with from the early days of a business. Foremost is to have a signed agreement with anyone who works at the company. Make sure they sign an NDA and an IP assignment agreement. Hiring employees, either full time or part time, is a complicated process. You should consult with your lawyer and accountant before hiring someone. You must be aware of the laws and requirements, such as minimum wage, benefits, withholding taxes, and so forth. You need to have a payroll system to pay wages. A business that has employees is responsible for paying federal, state, and social security taxes and other deductions. Usually, banks offer business services like payroll that you can subscribe to for a fee. At the end of the year, the company must issue W2 forms to employees. Nowadays, online payroll systems are very versatile, and an entrepreneur can do most of the work herself, but she still needs to know the laws and obligations.

Hiring contractors or advisors is a different case. It is simpler than hiring a full-time employee. You are not responsible for withholding taxes or offering benefits. Usually, you pay them an agreed upon amount for the service they provide. They are responsible for paying their own taxes and taking care of matters like health insurance. At the end of the year, you must report the payments to IRS on forms 1096 and issue 1099-MISC forms to contractors. Keep in mind that you will most likely be penalized by IRS and state authorities if you miscategorize a person who works for you. There are clear distinctions between an employee and a contractor.

In addition to monetary compensation, employees are usually offered an equity incentive. Be very careful about the structure and vesting plan as they may have unexpected tax ramifications. Some companies offer stock options that vest over time, say 25% every year. Another approach that has become popular is for companies to offer fully vested shares from the beginning but reserves the right to buy back a portion of them if the employee is terminated or leaves the company. For example, if the vesting period is four years, the employee will have all the equity incentives from the beginning. However, if he leaves after two years, he is only entitled to 50% of the promised equity; in the buyback mechanism, the company collects the other half.

Forming and managing a stock option pool for employees is something that must be done by an experienced attorney. It's a bad idea to try to do it yourself. It is a complicated task, and a professional who knows all the legal aspects of the process should manage the pool. It is also highly advisable to engage your accountant in the process to make sure the tax ramifications are well understood, and you have taken care of them.

Firing Employees

Although the best practice is to hire people who are a good fit regarding skill sets and culture, letting individuals go is an inevitable part of running a business. It is critical to include and specify in the contract that the employment is "at will." This clause protects the business from possible liabilities. Always assume that somewhere down the road you may part with an employee for any reason. It happens all the time, no matter how valuable someone is to the business at the date of hire. If the employment is "at will" (this must be spelled out in the employment agreement), you can easily let go of the employee with or without advance notice. It can be for any reason or no reason as long as you don't break the law. For example, dismissal based on unlawful discrimination is problematic. "At will" employment is a two-way street and employees can quit any time, with or without prior notice.

Aside from administrative and legal procedures, it is always good to part with people on reasonable terms. Typically, and especially in the U.S., employers prefer to do it quickly and have the employee leave the premises after being notified of his termination. The argument for escorting the employee off company premises is the fear of irrational reactions and doing damage to the company, like erasing or copying data. In most cases, being let go is an unpleasant experience for an employee and hurts his or her feelings and sometimes their pride. Doing it in a humane way is a good practice. Unless there is a good reason, it is better to think it over and avoid rashly firing people. I strongly recommend consulting with experienced entrepreneurs to see how you can minimize the negative impact. Briefly explaining the reason and thanking the employee for their service are good practices. Offering them a severance package is a thoughtful gesture if the company can afford it. Also, never lose perspective and forget that a leader bears responsibility for bringing out the best in his team.

Motivating Your Team

It is your responsibility to demand hard work and performance. However, another primary responsibility for a founder is to motivate the team and keep morale high. It is good practice to be transparent with the team, although that doesn't mean you have to share everything that is not related to their job. First, you must be careful and not overwhelm them with ever-changing information and details about the business that are not directly related to them. You need to create a sense of stability and consistency in the company. It is hard to run a productive team if the founders stress out about negative news and pass it directly to their employees.

A good leader implements an open-door policy and makes sure it is safe for everyone to freely express their opinions and ask questions. Creating a mindful and productive environment is crucial to the long-term prosperity of the business. You should schedule regular all-hands meetings, and discuss status, the latest progress and challenges. That is a great opportunity for the team to interact with leadership and learn about how the company is doing. Even if you have a small team, it's still good practice.

Motivating and encouraging the team is an art that can be learned. You should praise and give credit whenever it is due; don't shy away from it. Undoubtedly, a motivated team punches higher and strives for success. They go the extra mile to make things happen. They become your company's best ambassadors, and they can help attract other talent and even bring in customers. Never underestimate the value of motivation and drive. Finally, I believe a good work/life balance increases productivity. Let your employees have outside lives.

Office Space

Many famous startups originated in garages. The idea is not to spend money for an office before you reach a certain scale. In some areas, the cost of renting an office space is not high, and it may make sense to get a small room. However, in places like San Francisco or New York, the cost of renting an office before having any serious funding can be prohibitive. Nowadays there are alternatives such as coffee shops or co-working spaces. The benefit of renting a desk or space at a co-working office is to have a designated spot to work at every day. Also, the provider usually offers some refreshments and necessary equipment like printers and high-speed Wi-Fi. They are typically less noisy compared to coffee shops, and you have the benefit of working alongside other entrepreneurs.

You may find it hard to afford a spot at a co-working place. In this case, and as a short-term solution, the local library or a coffee shop might be a good choice. You can even make your cell phone a hotspot and use that for connecting to the Internet if your work is not data-heavy. These days cellular carriers offer good data plans. A personal hotspot is more secure than public Wi-Fi. As a rule of thumb, don't spend much on office space in the early days and before securing some capital. There is a reason for starting out of a garage, and as an entrepreneur, you shouldn't ignore that.

Business Cards

In the age of LinkedIn and all sorts of smartphone apps, one might think traditional business cards are outdated. On the contrary, they are still favored and useful. No one pulls out their smartphone and looks up your profile when they meet you for the first time. On the other hand, people can get a quick idea about you and your business by looking at a business card. And, most likely they will check out your profile and website after exchanging business cards. They're relatively inexpensive ($25 or less for 500 cards). It leaves a good impression if you print some for yourself and your business partners. Besides your name, title, basic contact info (email and phone number), and your company's name, you should add the website and location as well. You can easily design and order cards online.

Intuitive Entrepreneurship

Chapter Seven

Next Steps

Pivot

Changing course, or adjusting direction, is inevitable when you move forward with a startup. Building a business is a dynamic and ever-changing process. You are chasing a moving target which sometimes moves quite fast. You will lose your edge or competitive advantage if you don't adapt or "pivot." In the course of building a company, a wide variety of reasons can warrant a pivot.

In technology startups, often the need for a change comes when the entrepreneur faces insurmountable technological barriers in building the envisioned product. Imagine a startup company which is trying to build a quantum computer. Today, this is one of the most difficult technical tasks to accomplish. Engineers and researchers must solve complicated problems and fight the limits of physics. Operating at cryogenic temperatures helps to circumvent some of the fundamental obstacles, but still many are left to be solved. Such a startup company may not be able to address all the problems due to limited resources or critical barriers. However, they may pivot to a different product and market, based on a technology that they have developed in their quest to build a quantum computer.

Sometimes the market shifts and your product is left without a big enough customer base. At such times you need to be quick and reinvent your company. Adjusting your products and market strategies is imperative. Market shift is one of the main reasons that many companies, big or small, fail. Kodak is the classic example of how a market shift can doom your business. The rise of digital cameras put the last nails in the coffin of film-based photography. A recent example is Jawbone, Inc. which went into liquidation in 2017. Jawbone was a top maker of compact wireless earbuds. As the market shifted they pivoted to wearables, but they couldn't pull it off. Market shift is a significant threat and bring doom to a business if it doesn't execute a successful pivot.

Even if there is a need for your solution, the cost of the end product could be prohibitive. A business can get traction when its target customers are willing to pay for the product. Otherwise, revenue can't grow, and the penetration rate remains dismal. Another barrier could be the cost of development to bring commercial samples to the market. Before getting to the market, a startup may come short on capital and find no one willing to invest more in the business to help them get there. Entrepreneurs should anticipate this situation and make a pivot before running out of cash.

There are many stories in the startup world about successful pivots that changed the course of a company; there are even more examples of companies that failed to pivot successfully and went belly up. One of my favorite examples is Twitter, which pivoted from a podcast platform to what it is today. Pivoting is an essential part of entrepreneurship. As much as you should stay persistent and focused, you also must be agile and ready to change course if needed. It is a balancing act, one which requires sharp judgment and sense of direction.

There is a good chance that you will pivot at some point. At an early stage, you may discover that the market is not enthusiastic about your product. Or later, due to market dynamics and changing circumstances, you might find that the market has shifted. Whatever the reason, a wise entrepreneur doesn't hesitate to pivot when the time comes.

Scaling and Growth

If everything goes well and your team successfully executes, the company will enter the scaling and growth phase before long. The beginning of this phase is typically marked by a Series B funding. That is the time when the company must expand quickly and capture market share. The product is proven, refined, and has already hit the market. You have started riding the early adoption curve and are gearing up to ramp production or expand the service. The game plan shifts from building a viable product to dominating the market. When you enter the scaling phase, you have to adopt new strategies and execution plans. That is why you should constantly learn and educate yourself.

Overcoming Adversity

We began this book with a lesson from my experience training for and participating in triathlons. We also heard a few other stories. I'd like to leave you with another important lesson that I learned, and I am sure it will serve you well.

When I was training with Team in Training, Brian, our cycling coach, had a fantastic motto that helped us get through times of hardship, misfortunes, and mental barriers. His magic, three-word phrase was: "I Overcome Adversity." Time and time again, I invoked this motto and pulled myself through difficult situations. When you compete in triathlons, it is likely that you'll have a flat tire, a malfunctioning gear, muscle fatigue, and much more. Brian always reminded us that we should fight through it. I still have the inspirational wristbands that he made for all of us with "I Overcome Adversity" etched on them.

This motto resonates so much when you embark on starting a business. There are days when you feel helpless and disheartened. There are times when things don't move forward, no matter how hard you try. There are sleepless nights that seem never ending as you struggle to fix a problem. There are many occasions on which you are turned down by investors or potential customers. There are times when finances don't add up and the burden becomes so heavy that you don't see any way out. And there might come a day when you have to shut the whole operation down. In any of these situations, just stay focused on overcoming adversity. Entrepreneurship is an endurance sport and success depends very much on your mental strength; you must learn to be tough and resilient. At the same time, I'll bet you are going to have a lot of excitement and fun. It is gratifying to form a team, make a product that solves a real problem, and build a thriving business.

Finally, I hope this book gave you valuable insights about entrepreneurship and helped you understand the process. I encourage you to read more but don't forget that action and execution matter the most. Best of luck!

Further Reading

There are many books about entrepreneurship in circulation. Some authors recount their personal stories. Others tell you how hard it is to start a business. A few promise to make you a celebrity entrepreneur. Another group of writers tries to inspire readers to become entrepreneurs. Some investors write about how you can please them if you want to raise money from them. But among many books that I have read about entrepreneurship and innovation, there are a select few that I would like to mention here for further reading.

"The Startup Owner's Manual," by Steve Blank, is a classic manual which you can refer to on a variety of topics. The book is a reference and not necessarily something to read from the beginning to the end at once. Steve also has an excellent online course titled "How to Build a Startup" on Udacity.com that you can watch for free.

Morten T. Hansen's "Great by Choice" is an interesting book that gives readers a perspective on traits shared by successful companies. He finds common habits among prosperous and resilient businesspeople. I especially liked the concept of firing bullets and then firing cannonballs, which in short means you shouldn't dedicate all your resources and go all in before identifying the target.

"Venture Deals," by Brad Feld and Jason Mendelson, is a comprehensive look at term sheets and details of contracts with potential investors. A term sheet is a convoluted document and has many elements to protect and maximize an investor's interests. As an entrepreneur, you may end up with an unfavorable deal if not familiar with the details. We discussed some of the key features in my book, but "Venture Deals" is a good book to read before you sign an agreement with investors.

I read "The Narrow Road, A Brief Guide to the Getting of Money," by Felix Dennis, a few years ago and some of his comments have stuck in my head. He covers different aspects of making money in 88 short sections. It is a pleasant read, and you likely will find useful takeaways.

"Draw to Win," by Dan Roam, is a good read if you want to improve your drawing skills for business presentations. It is an enjoyable and useful book that helps you deliver a message effectively with drawings and figures.

Appendix A

Sample Executive Summary

Accurate Techniques, Inc.
Seed Round - Summer 2017

Early-stage startup based in SF developing wearable coaches. New technology with multiple sensors that helps users acquire pro-level skills/technique in any sport and achieve their best performance by tracking and modeling their movement, receiving live feedback.

Pain Point: All athletes and sports enthusiasts know how valuable a holistic view and live feedback are to take their technique to the next level and achieve their best performance. No product in the market can accurately monitor movement and provide valuable quantitative analytics and coaching. Currently, acquiring proper technique in any sport is a cumbersome, painful, expensive, and lengthy process.

Solution: A wearable device with multiple sensors tracks essential body movements, models patterns, determines the efficiency and accuracy of the technique, and provides live coaching and feedback. A vast array of analytics provides unparalleled insights and feedback, such as detailed analysis, coaching, and comparison of a user's technique to pro athletes.

Customers: Athletes and sports enthusiasts.

Market: Wearables are on track to become a $50+ billion market. Our goal is to dominate the market for wearable coaches, which covers subcategories like sports coaches, medical coaches, and sleep coaches.

Competition: Mainly focused on general-purpose-single-sensor devices that are either geared toward fitness/health for the general public or mounted on sports equipment. None is specialized in multi-sensor wearable coaches. Competitive products are passive and do not provide a holistic view of an athlete's movements or give live and active coaching/feedback about technique.

Unfair Advantage: Compact and lowest power solution in the market, plus a sophisticated algorithm for accurately modeling an athlete's technique.

Business Model: Potential sources of revenue: 1) selling hardware, i.e., wearables; 2) subscriptions for online services. Expected revenue of $50 Million in three years with annual growth of 30-50%.

Go-to-Market Strategy: In the beginning, we will go after a few popular sports with the highest impact and ROI, such as golf, with 30 million, mostly affluent players in the United States. Other early adopters are triathlon/Ironman athletes who have an insatiable appetite for new technologies. Next, we expand to international markets, and cover 60+ million runners, 65+ million cyclists, and 80+ million swimmers in the U.S.

Financing: Seeking $600,000 in seed investment for 12 months to get to the beta version.

Team:
John Smith
Co-founder/CEO & System Architect

10 years of experience at top Silicon Valley startups. Ph.D. in Electrical Engineering, Columbia University.

Emma Chang
Co-founder & Lead Software Engineer
8 years of solid track record at top-tier tech companies. MS in Computer Science, Stanford University.

Mark Shepard
Lead Algorithm Designer
8 years of experience in Silicon Valley companies. MS in Electrical Engineering, Carnegie Mellon University.

(Advisor) **Alex Green**, Founder/CEO, Sports Props, Inc.

(Advisor) **Heather West,** experienced Ironman and sports coach

CONFIDENTIAL

john@AccurateTechnique.com | (415) 000-0000

Appendix A

www.ingramcontent.com/pod-product-compliance
Lightning Source LLC
Chambersburg PA
CBHW031623210526
45464CB00004B/1724